PIANO · VOCAL · GUITAR

THE BIG BOOK OF

DISCO & FUNK

ISBN 0-634-04597-0

HAL·LEONARD® CORPORATION

7777 W. BLUEMOUND RD. P.O. BOX 13819 MILWAUKEE, WI 53213

Visit Hal Leonard Online at
www.halleonard.com

CONTENTS

BAD GIRLS

Words and Music by JOE "BEANS" ESPOSITO, EDWARD HOKENSON,
BRUCE SUDANO and DONNA SUMMER

BOOGIE NIGHTS

Words and Music by
ROD TEMPERTON

Fast Jazz feel

Boo - gie___ nights___

whoa,___ whoa.___

Boo - gie___ nights,___ whoa,___ whoa.___

Moderately fast Disco

Boo - gie nights.

Boo - gie nights.

(Boo - gie night.) Ain't no doubt | Get that groove; | It's all right

we are here to par - ty. | let it take you high - er. | when you've got the feel - ing.

(Boo - gie night.) Come on now, got to get it start - ed. | Make it move; set this place on fire. | Hold it tight; got to keep on deal - ing.

Dance with the boo - gie, get down,

(Dance with the boo - gie; get down.)

'cause boo - gie nights are

Got to keep on danc - ing, keep on danc - ing. Got to keep on danc - ing,

keep on danc - ing. (Boo - gie ___ night, ___ whoa, ___
(Do you wan - na boo - gie? Boo - gie, boo - gie, boo - gie

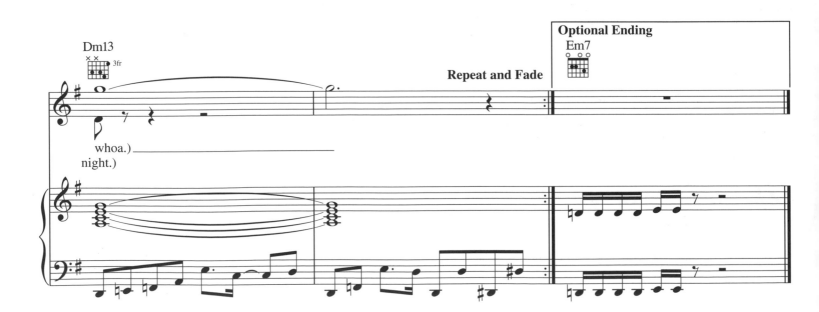

whoa.) ___
night.)

BOOGIE ON REGGAE WOMAN

Words and Music by
STEVIE WONDER

Moderate Funk

I like to see you boo-gie right a-cross the floor.
I'd like to see both of us fall deep-ly in love.
(Instrumental)

I like to do it to you till you hol-ler for more.
I'd like to see you and me un-der the stars a-bove.

Spoken: Yes, I would.

I'd like to Reg-gae
I'd like to see both of us

BOOGIE OOGIE OOGIE

Words and Music by JANICE MARIE JOHNSON
and PERRY KIBBLE

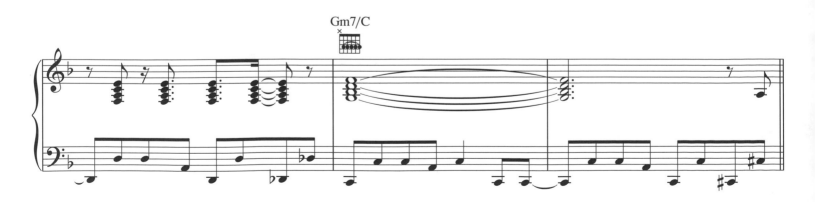

If you're think - ing you're__ too cool_____ to boog -
There's no time__ to waste;__ let's get the show on the road.__

- ie,

boy oh boy, have I__
Lis - ten to the mu - sic and__

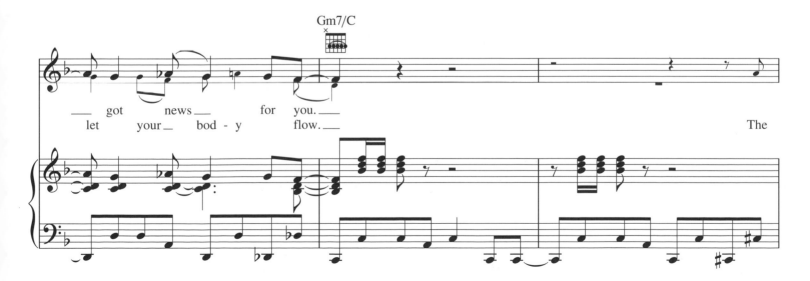

__ got news__ for you.__
let your__ bod - y flow.__

The

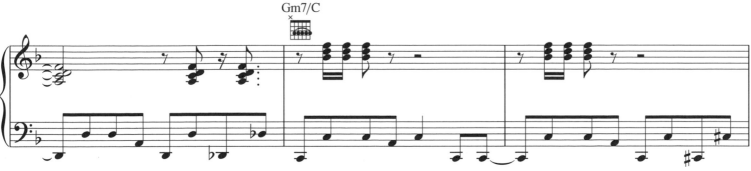

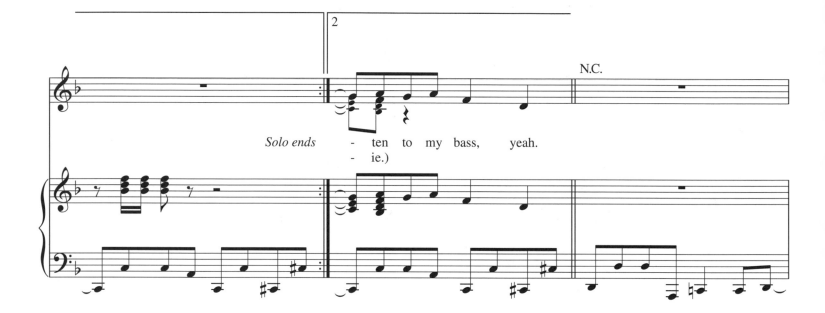

Solo ends - ten to my bass, yeah.

(- ie.)

N.C.

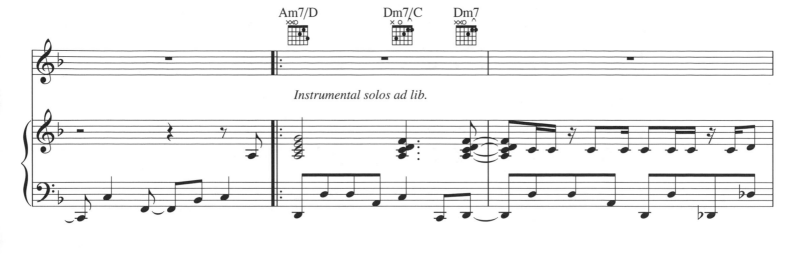

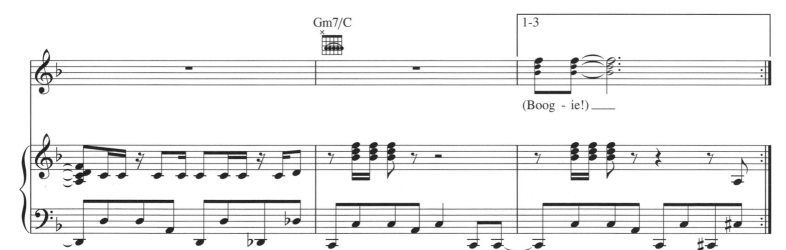

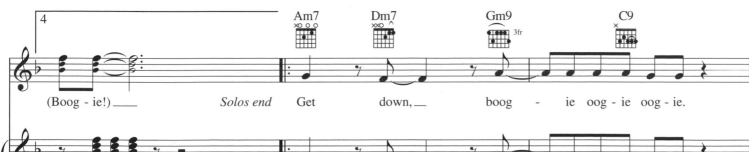

BOOGIE WONDERLAND

Words and Music by JON LIND
and ALLEE WILLIS

You say__ your__ prayers__ though you don't care;__ you__ dance__ and shake

D.S. % al Coda

the hurt._____

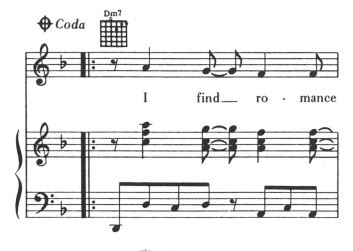

⊕ *Coda*

I find__ ro - mance

when I__ start to dance__ in Boo - gie Won - der - land.

All__ the__ love in the world can't be__ gone.

All_____ the need to be loved can't be wrong.

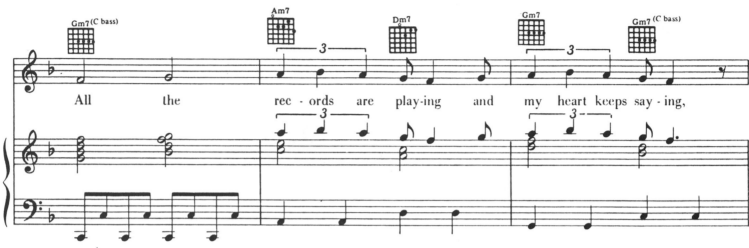

All the rec-ords are play-ing and my heart keeps say - ing,

"Boo - gie Won - der - land,_____ Won - der -

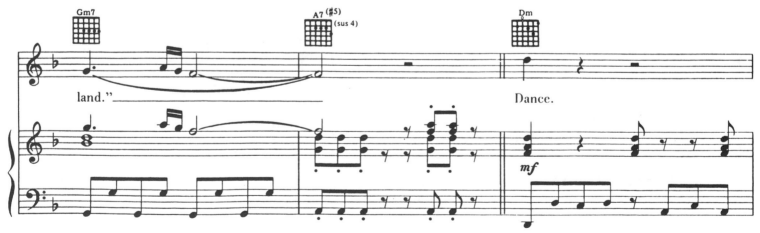

land."_____ Dance.

Boo - gie Won - der - land. _____ Ha, ha,

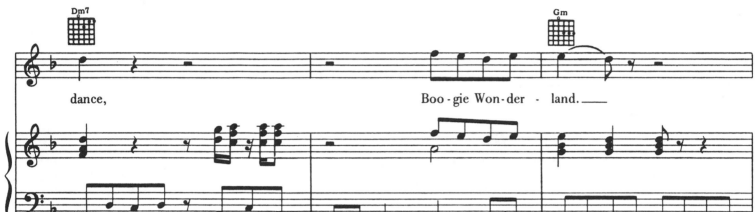

dance, Boo - gie Won - der - land. _____

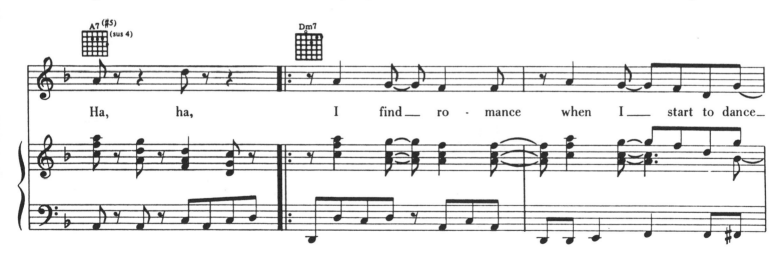

Ha, ha, I find _____ ro - mance when I _____ start to dance _____

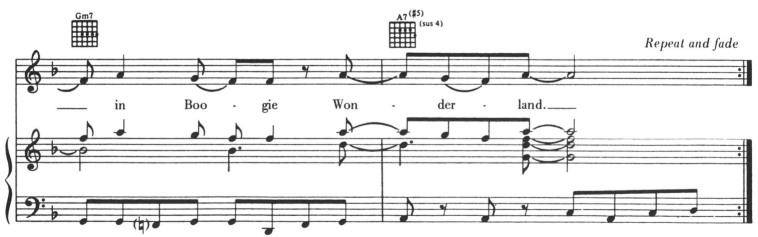

Repeat and fade

_____ in Boo - gie Won - der - land. _____

BRICK HOUSE

Words and Music by LIONEL RICHIE, RONALD LaPREAD,
WALTER ORANGE, MILAN WILLIAMS,
THOMAS McCLARY and WILLIAM KING

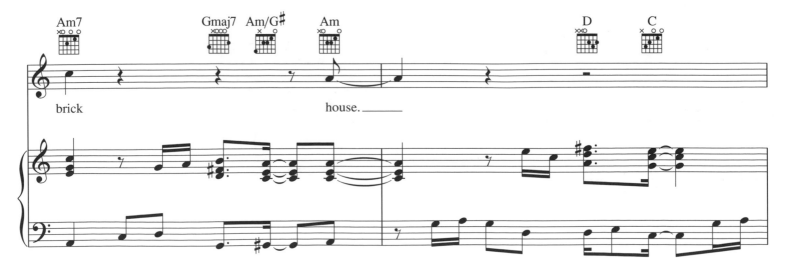

She's might - y, might - y, just let - tin' it all ___ hang out. ___ Ah, she's a

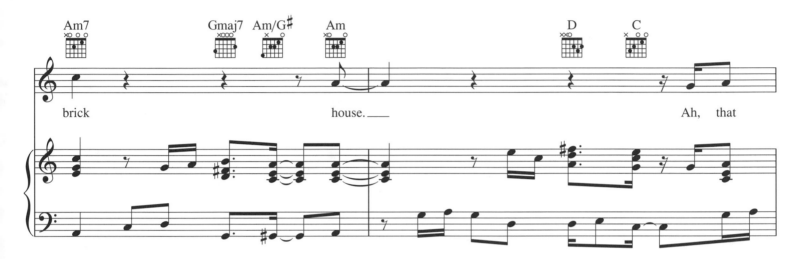

brick house. ___ Ah, that

la - dy's stacked ___ and that's a fact, ___ ain't hold - in' noth - in' back. ___ Ow, she's a

brick house. ___ Well,

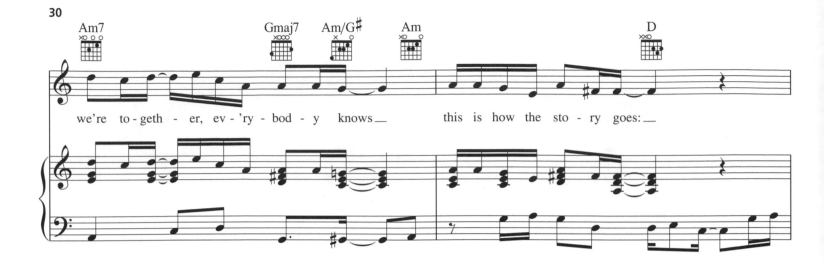

we're to-geth - er, ev-'ry-bod - y knows ___ this is how the sto - ry goes: ___

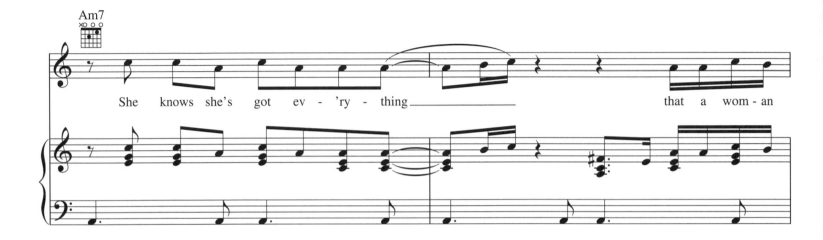

She knows she's got ev - 'ry - thing ___ that a wom - an

needs to get a man, yeah, yeah. How can she lose ___ with the

stuff she use? Thir - ty - six, twen - ty - four, ___ thir - ty - six!

Oh, what a win-ning hand,___ 'cause she's a brick house.___

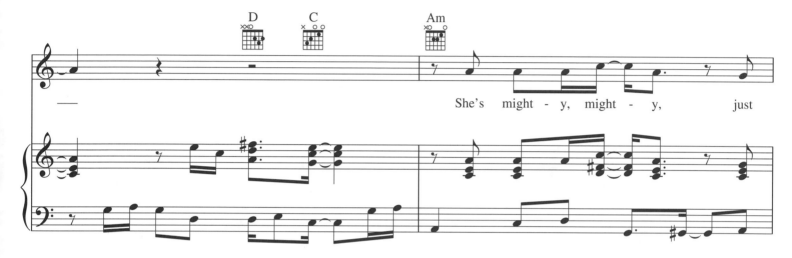

___ She's might-y, might-y, just

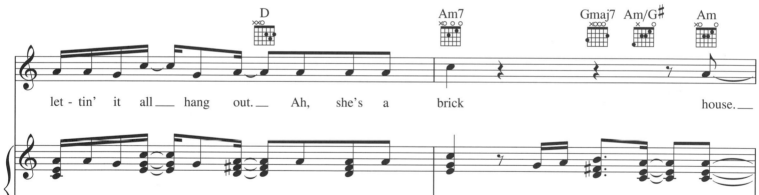

let-tin' it all___ hang out.___ Ah, she's a brick house.___

___ Ow,___ that la-dy's stacked___ and that's a fact,___

ain't hold-in' noth-in' back.___ Oh, she's a brick___ house,___

___ yeah._____ She's the one,___ the on-ly one,___

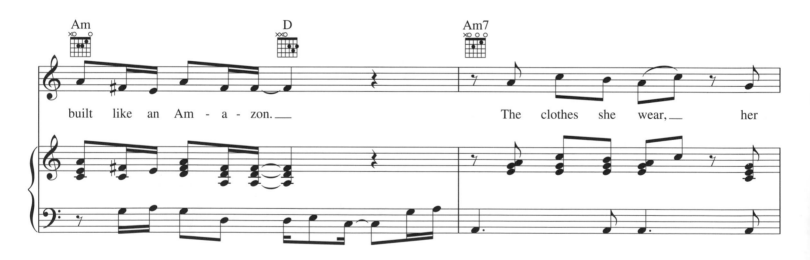

built like an Am-a-zon.___ The clothes she wear,___ her

sex-y ways___ make an old___ man___ wish for

young - er days, ___ yeah, yeah. She knows she's built and

knows how to please. ___ Sho' nuf can knock a strong ___

man to his knees, ___ 'cause she's a brick house. ___

Yeah, ___ she's might - y, might - y, ___ just

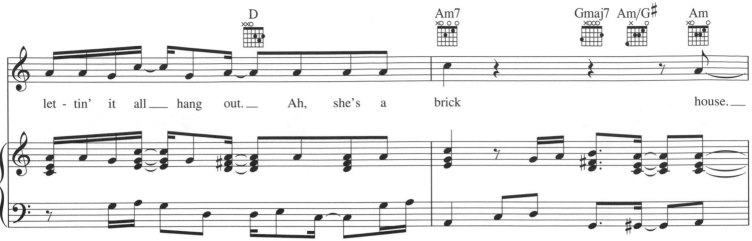

let - tin' it all ___ hang out. ___ Ah, she's a brick house. ___

That la - dy's stacked ___ and that's a fact, ___
Yeah, she's the one, ___ the on - ly one, ___

ain't hold - in' noth - in' back. ___ Ow!
built like an Am - a - zon. ___ Yeah!

Shook - a dow shook - a dow dow,

1-3

shook - a dow shook - a dow dow.

4

D.S. and Fade

shook - a dow shook - a dow.

COPACABANA
(At the Copa)

Music by BARRY MANILOW
Lyric by BRUCE SUSSMAN and JACK FELDMAN

Moderately, with a Latin feel

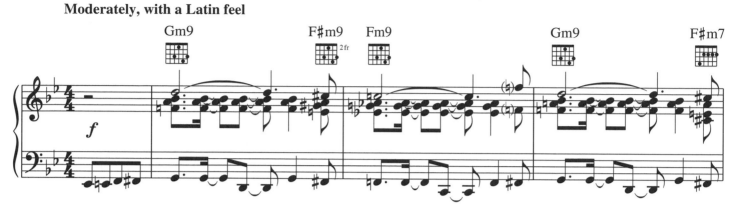

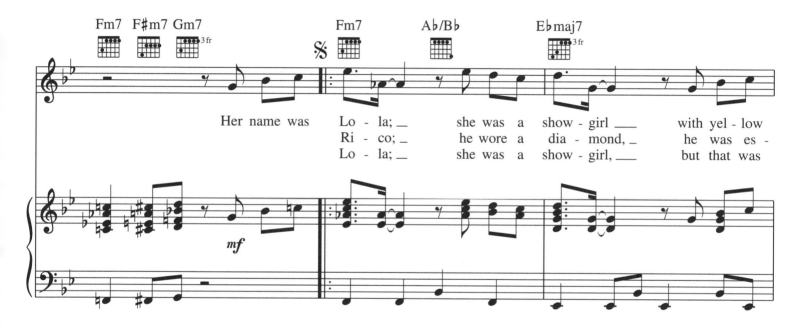

Her name was Lo-la; she was a show-girl with yel-low
Ri-co; he wore a dia-mond, he was es-
Lo-la; she was a show-girl, but that was

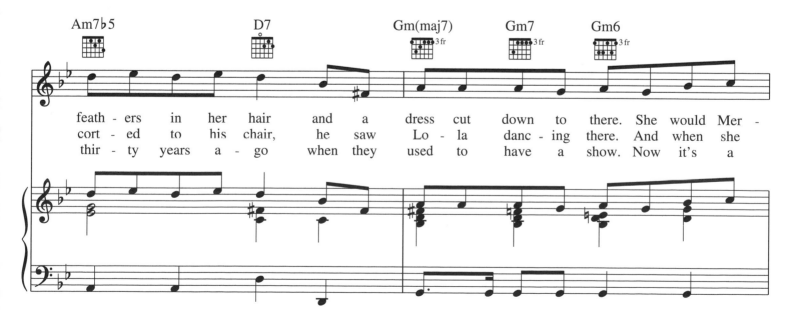

feath-ers in her hair and a dress cut down to there. She would Mer-
cort-ed to his chair, he saw Lo-la danc-ing there. And when she
thir-ty years a-go when they used to have a show. Now it's a

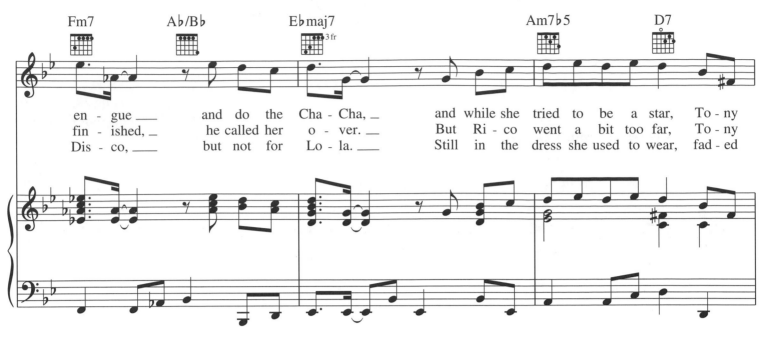

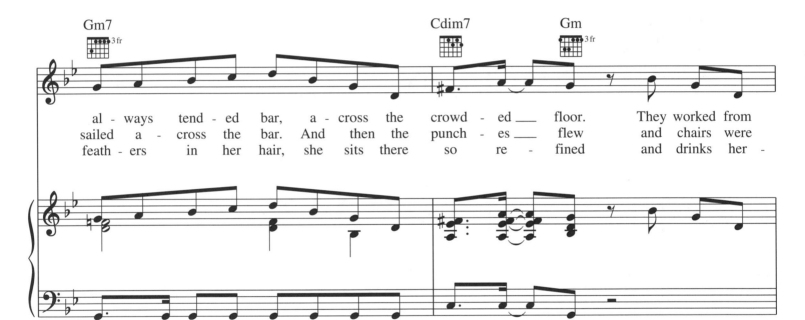

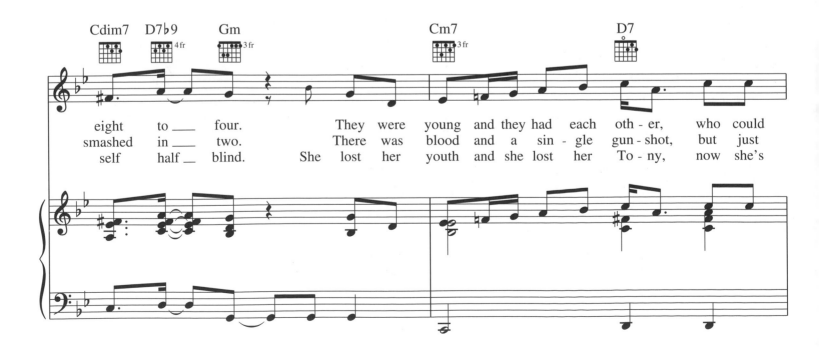

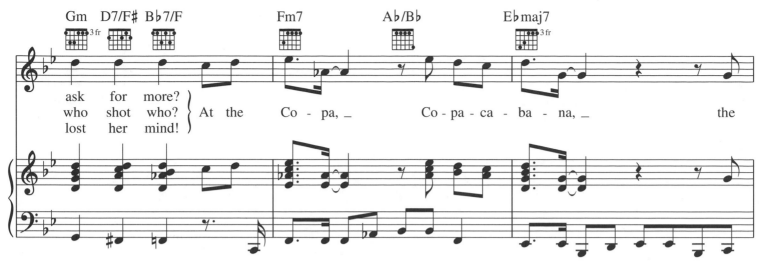

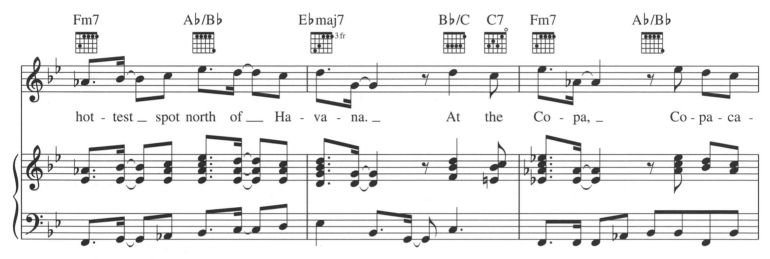

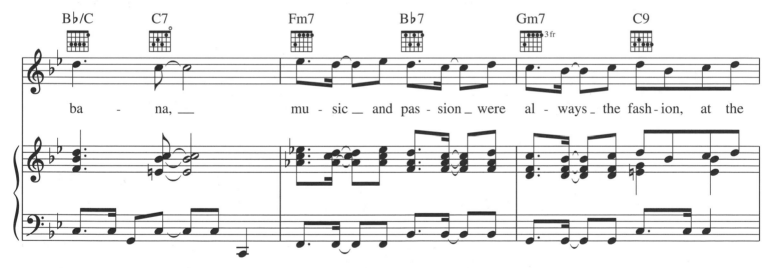

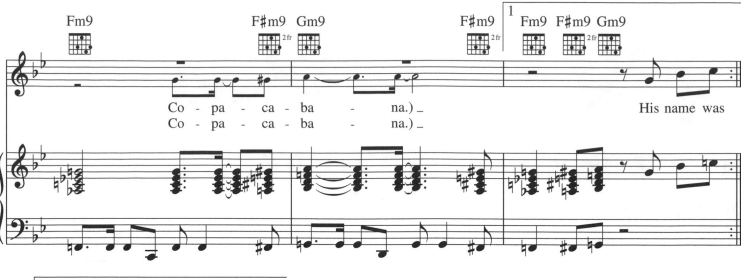

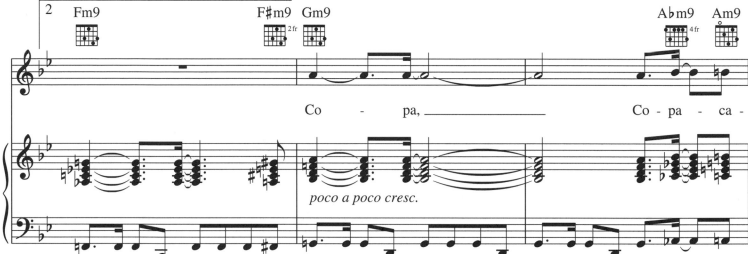

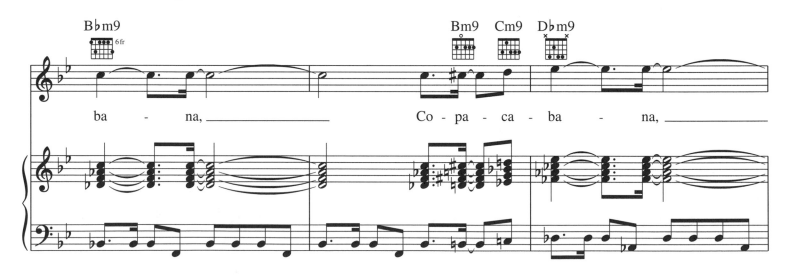

Ah, _____ Ah, _____

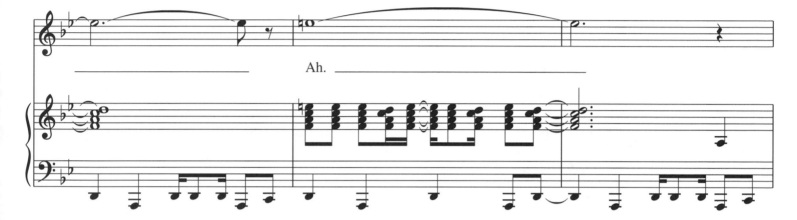

_____ Ah. _____

Ah. _____

Co - pa, _____ Co - pa - ca -

ba - na, _____ like in __ Ha - va - na, _____

_____ have a __ ba - na - na, _____ mu - sic __ and

pas - sion _____ al - ways _ in fash - ion.

Instrumental solo ad lib.

COLD SWEAT, PT. 1

Words and Music by JAMES BROWN
and ALFRED JAMES ELLIS

I don't care   a - bout your past, ___   I just
I don't care   a - bout your won'ts, ___   I just

want ___   our love to last. ___   I don't care
wan-na tell you ___   'bout your do's ___ and don'ts.   I don't care

a - bout your faults,   I just want ___
a - bout the way you treat me, dar - ling,   I just want ___

to sat - is - fy your thoughts.
to un - der - stand me al - ways.

When you kiss me, _____ when you miss me,

hold ___ my hand, _____ make me un - der - stand. ___

D.C.
D.C. and Fade

I wake up in a cold sweat!

DA YA THINK I'M SEXY

Words and Music by ROD STEWART
and CARMINE APPICE

Medium Disco beat

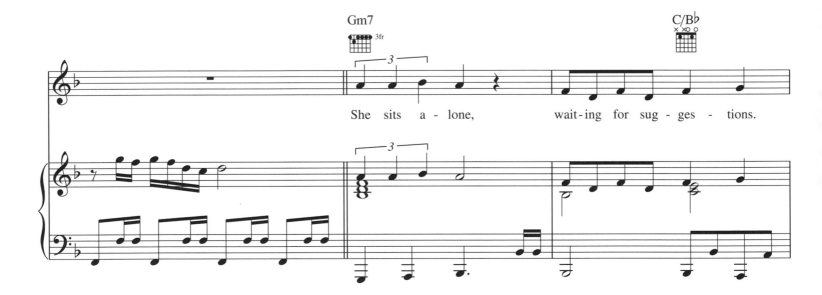

She sits a - lone, wait-ing for sug - ges - tions.

He's so nerv - ous; a - void-ing all the ques - tions.

His lips are dry, her heart is gen - tly pound - ing.

Don't you just know ex - act - ly what they're think - ing?___ If___

___ you want my bod - y and___ you think I'm sex - y, come___ on, sug - ar, let me know.___

If ___ you real - ly need me, just ___ reach out and touch me. Come___

on, hon - ey, tell me so.___ He's act - ing shy,
They wake at dawn, 'cause

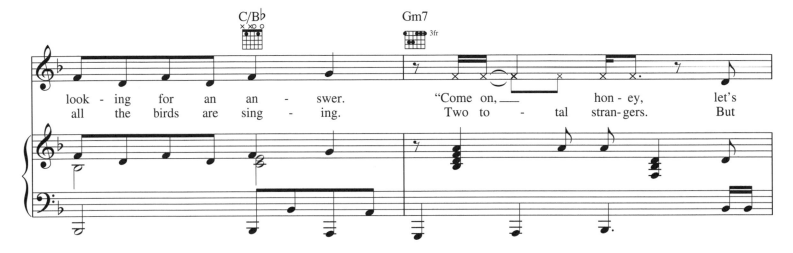

look - ing for an an - swer. "Come on,___ hon - ey, let's
all the birds are sing - ing. Two to - tal stran - gers. But

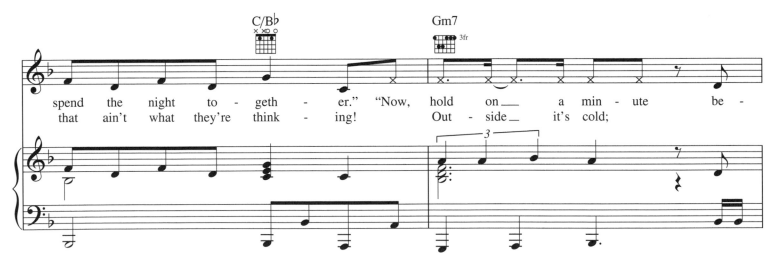

spend the night to - geth - er." "Now, hold on___ a min - ute be -
that ain't what they're think - ing! Out - side___ it's cold;

fore we go much fur - ther. Give me a dime, so I can phone my moth - er."
mist - y and it's rain - ing. They got each oth - er. Nei - ther one's com - plain - ing.

Gm7

They catch a cab_____ to his high - rise a - part - ment. At
He says, "I'm sor - ry, but I'm out of milk and cof - fee."

Gm7   **C/B♭**   **Dm7**

last____ he can tell her ex - act - ly what his heart meant.
"Nev - er mind,__ sug - ar. We can watch the ear - ly mov - ie." If _____ you want my bod - y and___

F

____ you think I'm sex - y, come__ on, sug - ar, let me know.__ If __

Dm7   **F**   **To Coda ⊕**

____ you real - ly need me, just____ reach out and touch me. Come__ on, hon - ey, tell me so.__

His heart's beat-ing like a drum, ___ 'cause at

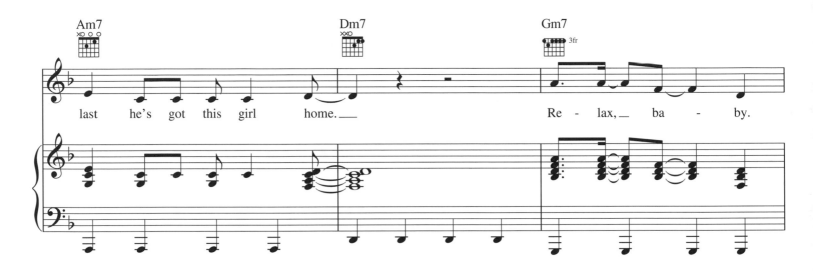

last he's got this girl home. ___ Re - lax, ___ ba - by.

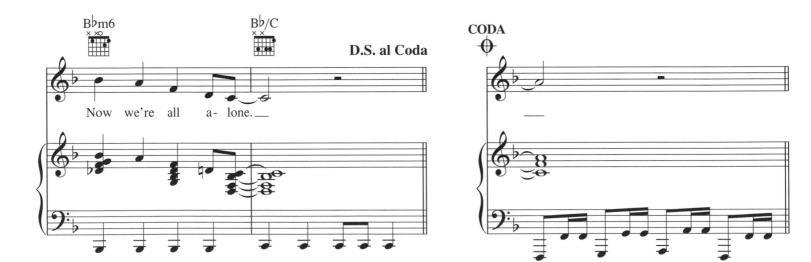

Now we're all a- lone. ___

D.S. al Coda

CODA

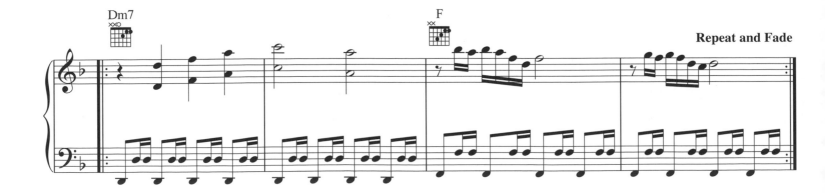

Repeat and Fade

DANCE WITH ME

Words and Music by PETER BROWN
and ROBERT RANS

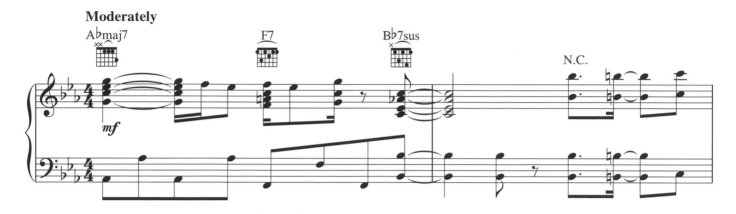

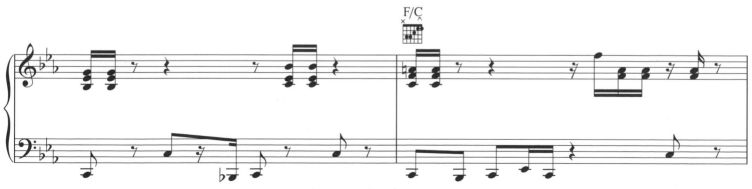

(Got - ta keep on mak - in' me high; __ you got - ta keep on mak - in' me high. __

Got - ta keep on mak - in' me high; __ you got - ta keep on mak - in' me high.) __

1.,3. If you're feel - ing sad and blue, __ come on __ and

2. La - dies, get up off your seats; __ come on __ and

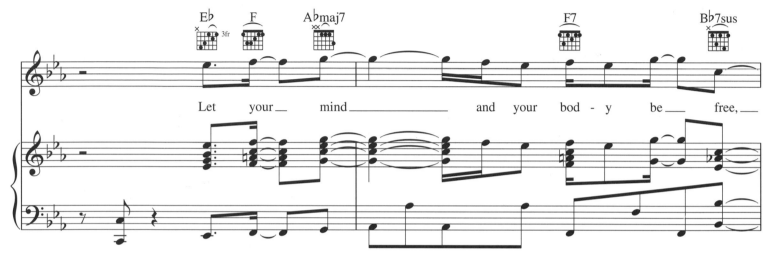

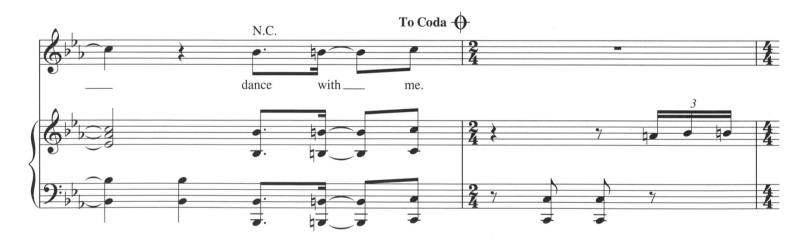

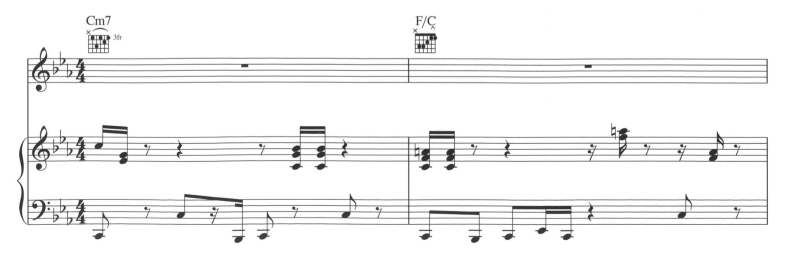

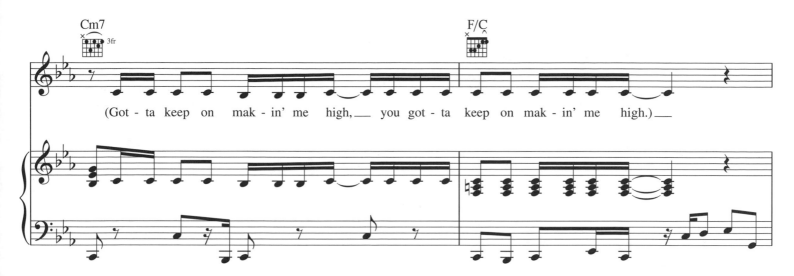

(Got - ta keep on mak - in' me high, __ you got - ta keep on mak - in' me high.) __

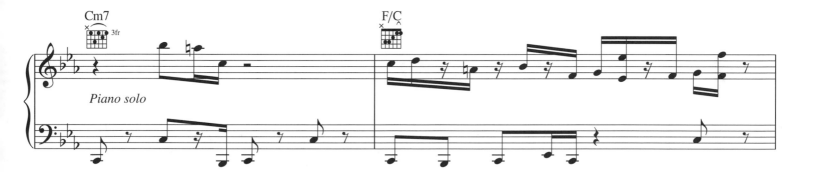

Piano solo

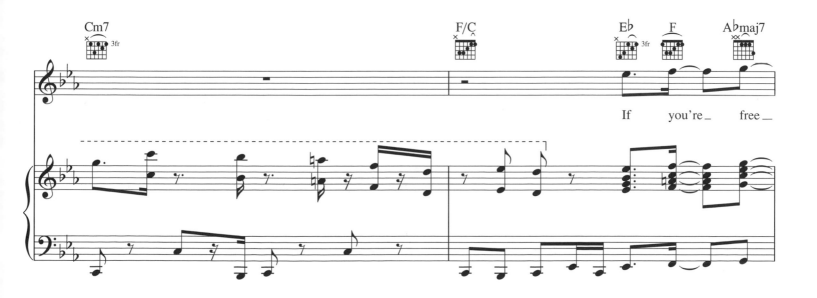

If you're _ free _

and you like what you ___ see, _____ dance with ___ me.

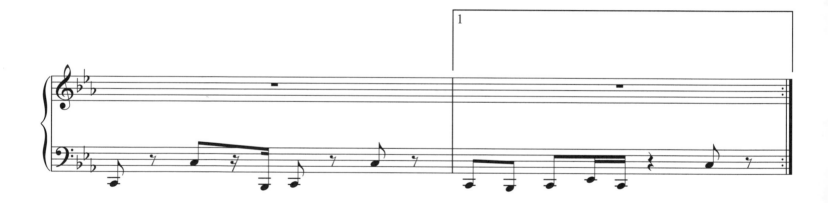

Female: You got to keep danc - in', 'cause it's mak - in' me high;__ you got - ta

(You got - ta keep on mak - in' me high; you got - ta
keep, keep danc - in'. You got to keep danc - in' 'cause it's mak - in' me high; you got - ta

keep on mak - in' me high.)
keep, keep danc - in'. You got to keep danc - in' 'cause it's mak - in' me high; you got - ta

(You got - ta keep on mak - in' me high; you got - ta

1–3

4

Eb F Abmaj7

keep on mak - in' me high.)
keep, keep danc - in'. You keep, keep danc - in',

keep on mak - in' me high.)
keep, keep danc - in',

F7

Bb7sus

N.C.

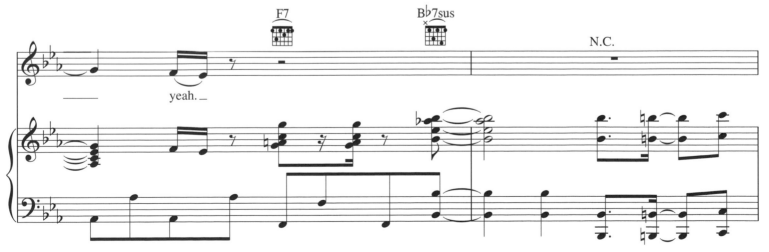

yeah.

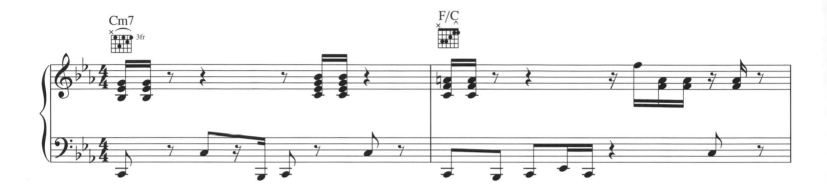

D.S. al Coda

(Got - ta keep on mak - in' me high;___ you got - ta keep on mak - in' me high.)___

CODA

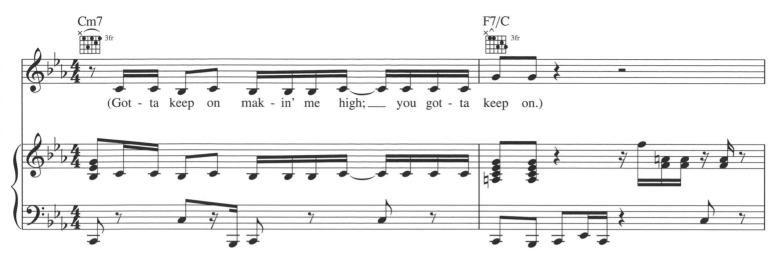

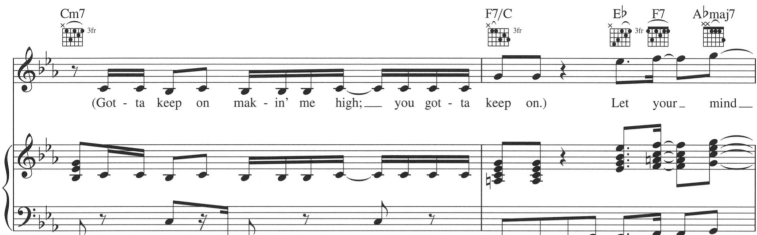

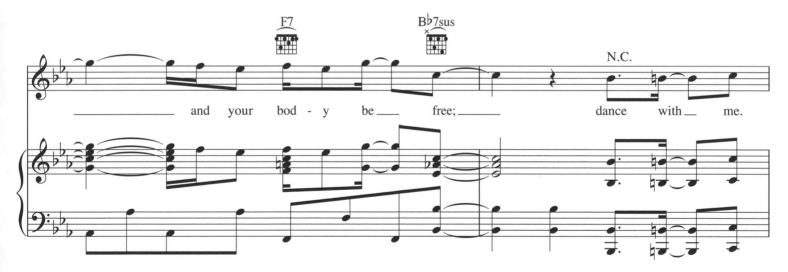

DO IT GOOD

Words and Music by JANICE MARIE JOHNSON
and PERRY KIBBLE

Funky Disco

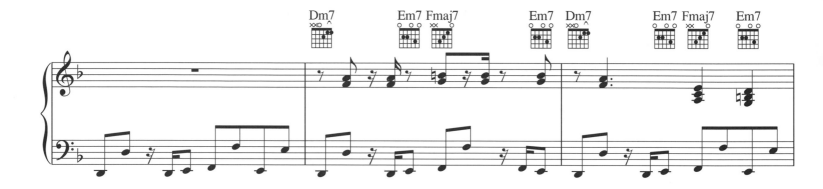

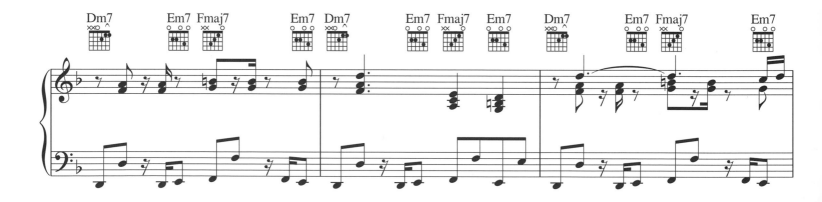

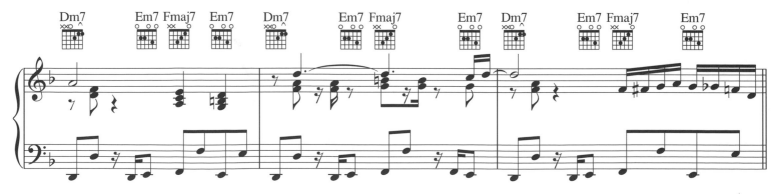

Original key: E♭ minor. This edition has been transposed down one half-step to be more playable.

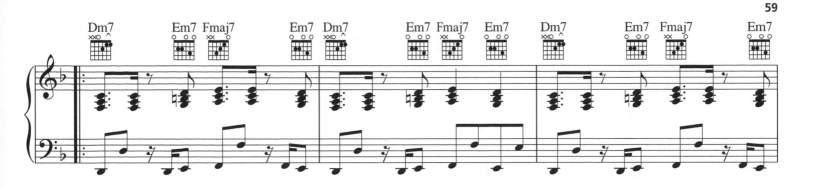

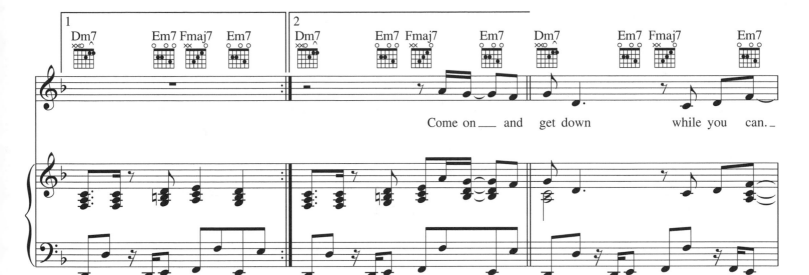

Come on ___ and get down ___ while you can. ___

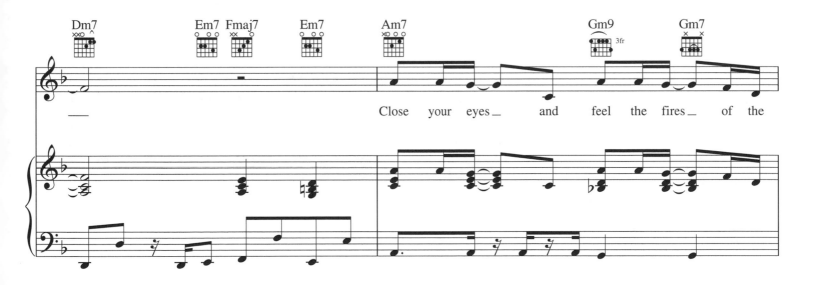

___ Close your eyes ___ and feel the fires ___ of the

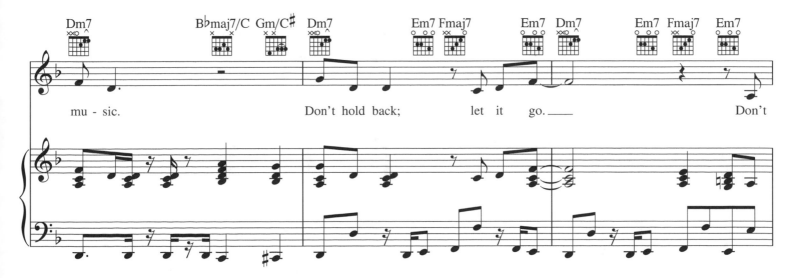

mu - sic. Don't hold back; let it go. ___ Don't

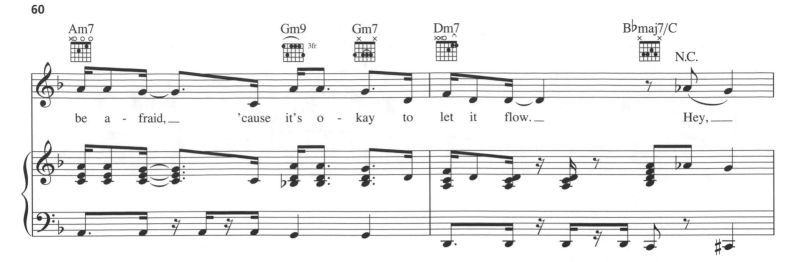

be a-fraid, __ 'cause it's o-kay to let it flow. __ Hey, __

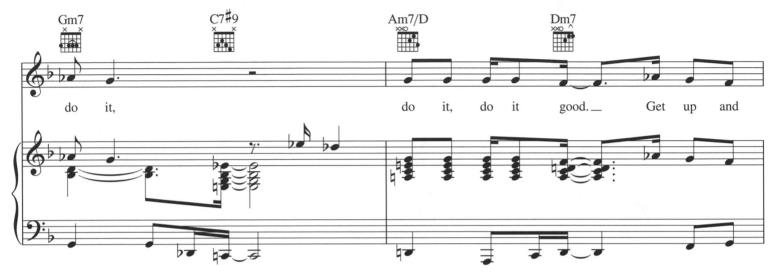

do it, do it, do it good. __ Get up and

do it, do it, do it good. __ Come on and

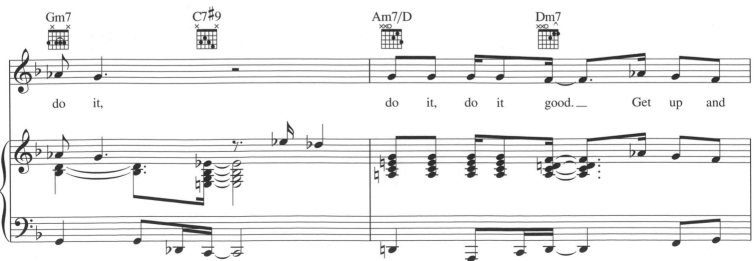

do it, do it, do it good. __ Get up and

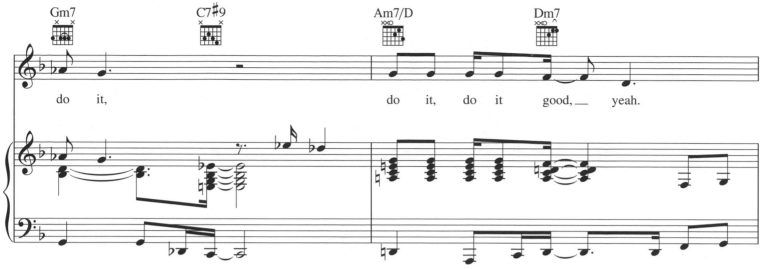

do it,   do it, do it good,   yeah.

Hmm,   hmm.

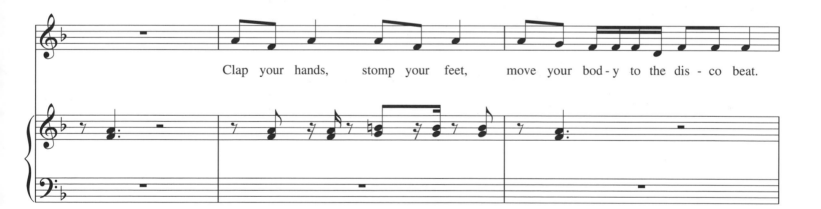

Clap your hands,   stomp your feet,   move your bod-y to the dis-co beat.

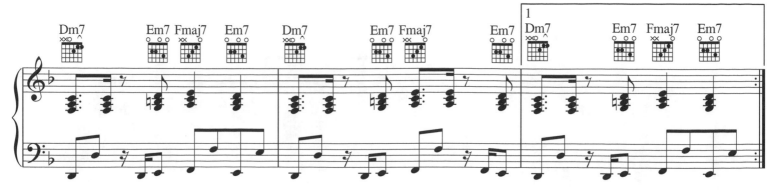

The stage __ is set now; the light's __ on __ you. _____

You can do __ it; get in-to __ it, feel it through and __ through. __

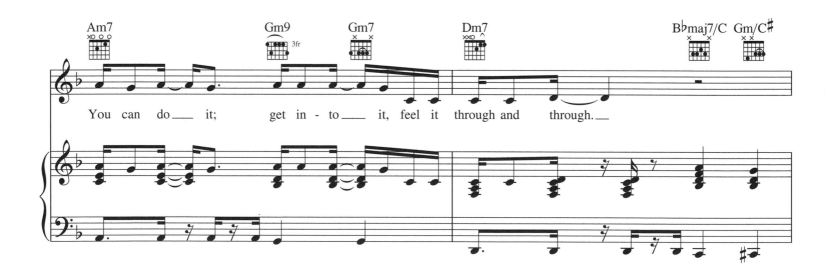

Don't be shy, get it on; _____ and put your

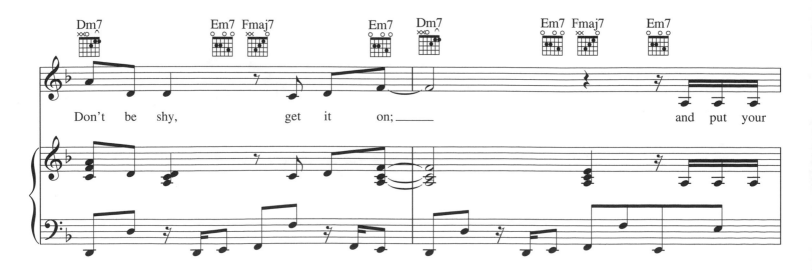

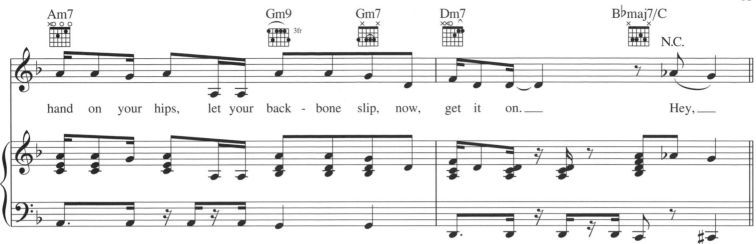

hand on your hips, let your back-bone slip, now, get it on.___ Hey, ___

do it, do it, do it good.___ Get up and do it,

do it, do it good.___ Come on and do it,

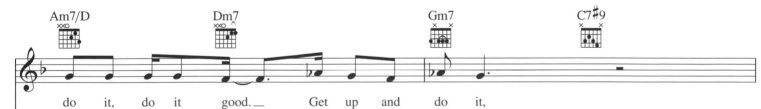

do it, do it good.___ Get up and do it,

do it, do it, ev - 'ry - bod - y, do it, do it good. ___

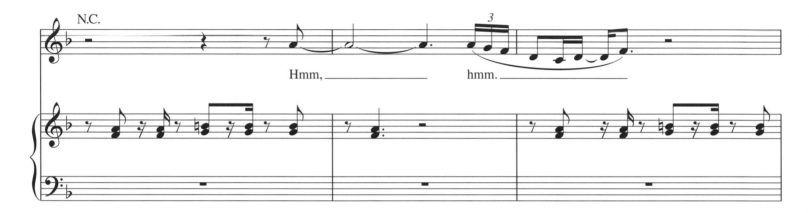

Hmm, _____ hmm. ___

Clap your hands, stomp your feet, move your bod - y to the freak - y beat.

Shake ___ it on down.

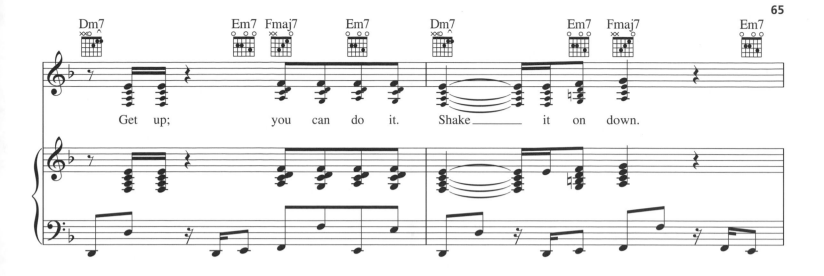

Get up; you can do it. Shake _____ it on down.

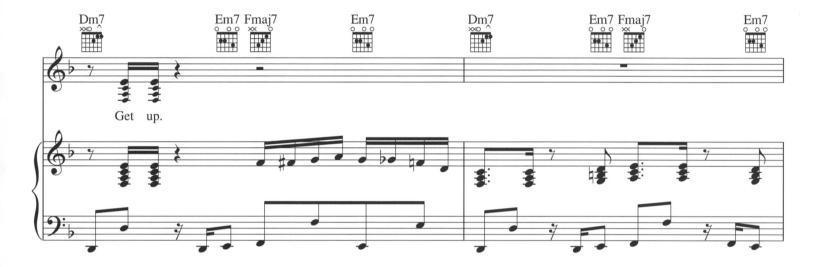

Get up.

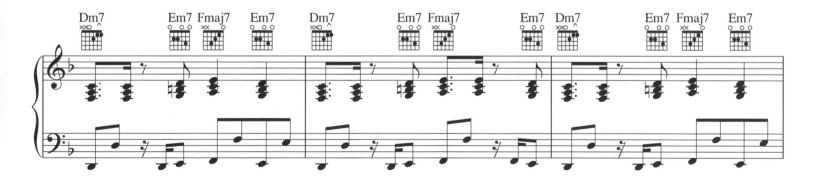

Ah, _____ you can do it. _____

DO YOU WANNA GET
FUNKY WITH ME

Words and Music by PETER BROWN
and ROBERT RANS

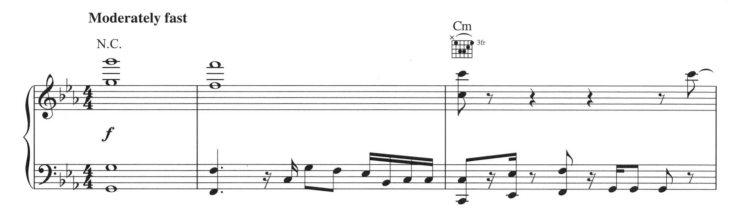

This edition has been transposed up one half-step to be more playable.

The la - dy smiled___ at me when she asked a - bout___ the pos - si - bil - i - ty

wan - na get funk - y with me? Do you wan - na?

(Do you wan - na get funk - y?) (Do you wan - na get funk - y?) (Do you wan - na get

funk - y?) (Do you wan - na get funk - y?) (Do you wan - na get funk - y with me?)

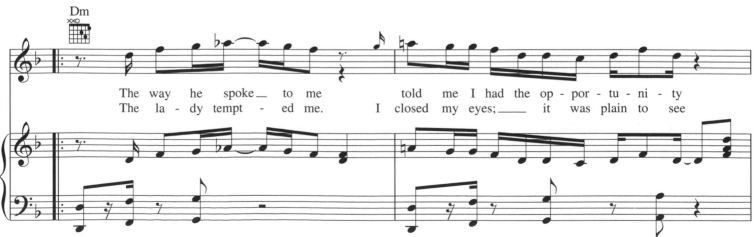

The way he spoke__ to me ___ told me I had the op - por - tu - ni - ty
The la - dy tempt - ed me. I closed my eyes;___ it was plain to see

to see how funk - y she could be. And
she was the dev - il in dis - guise. And

when I looked in - to her eyes, __ the fire they held made me re - al - ize __
oh, the mes - sage she'd re - lay __ when she would take my __ hand and say, __ "Do you

1
the flame was burn - ing just for me.

2
wan - na get funk - y with me?" (Do you wan - na?)

The i-dle mind___ is a play - ground for the dev - il. Do you

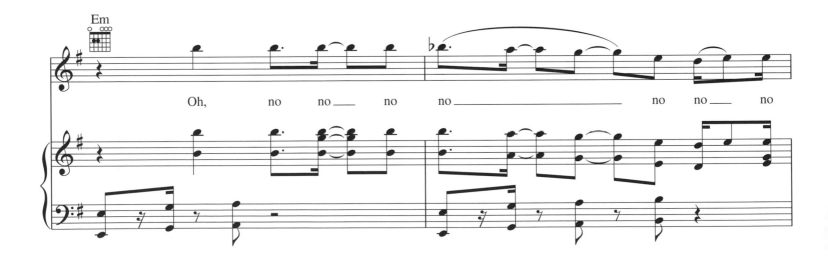

wan-na get funk-y with me? Do you wan-na?

Oh, no no___ no no_____ no no___ no

no____ no___ no_____ no.____

(I wan - na set you on fire,_____ 'cause it's hot

'cause it's hot___ 'cause it's hot.)

Em

I felt that heat_ with - in,___ the lust of love,_ and the urge_ to sin._

I felt her reach - in' for my soul._____ And

then I knew I had no choice but to heed the com-mand of the dev-il's voice: "Do you

(Do you wan-na? Do you wan-na? Do you wan-na?)

wan-na get funk-y with me? Do you wan-na? Do you wan-na?"

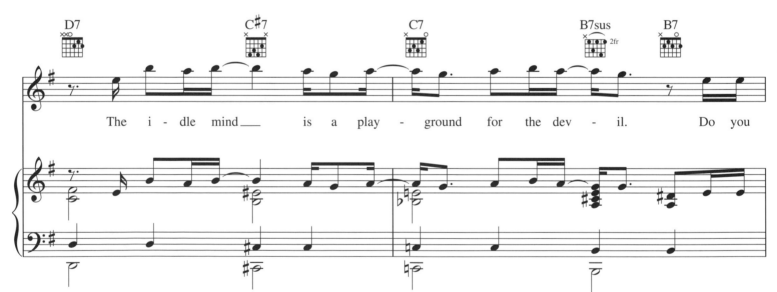

D7　　　　　C#7　　　　　C7　　　　　B7sus　B7

The i-dle mind is a play-ground for the dev-il. Do you

Em

wan-na get funk-y with me? Do you wan-na get funk-y? Mm. Do you

wan - na get funk - y with me? Do you wan - na?

The i - dle mind____ is a play - ground for the dev - il._____

Oh,_____ do you wan - na get funk - y with me? Do you wan - na?

Do you wan-na get funk - y with me?

DO THE FUNKY CHICKEN

Words and Music by
RUFUS THOMAS

Moderately fast

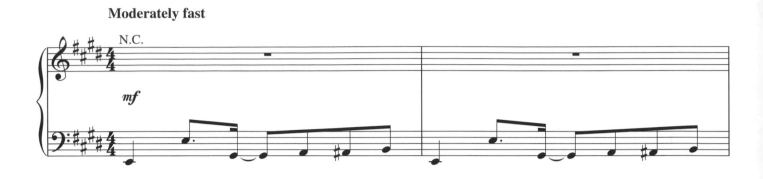

You put your

left arm up, right arm too. Let __
both arms up a - bove your face and your
work both arms and you work both feet. We to -

__ me tell you what you've got to do.
knees start wig - glin' __ all o - ver the place.
geth - er, ba - by. __ You right on the beat.

Flap your wings __ and your feet start kick - in'.

Then you know __ you're doin' __ the funk - y chick - en.

(Come on and do the funk - y chick - en.)

To Coda ⊕

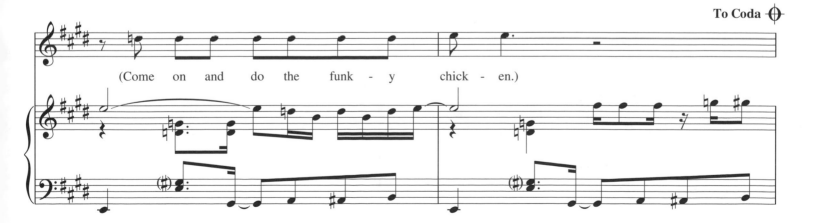

(Come on and do the funk - y chick - en.)

You put

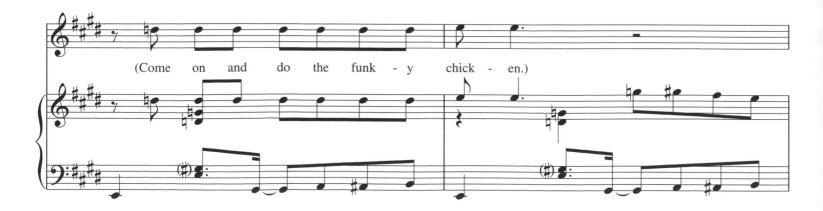

(Come on and do the funk - y chick - en.)

Y'all read - y

fel - las, y'all read - y fel - las, y'all read - y

fel - las, y'all read - y fel - las, y'all read - y

fel - las, y'all read - y fel - las, y'all read - y

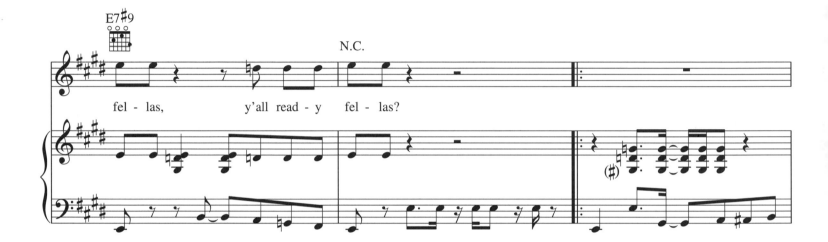

fel - las, y'all read - y fel - las?

1

2

Do __

the funk - y chick - en now. Do _____ the funk - y chick - en now.

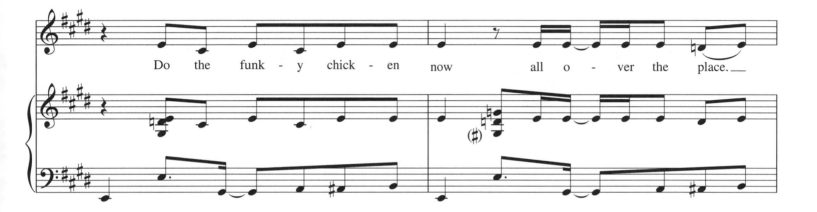

Do the funk - y chick - en now all o - ver the place. __

N.C.

D.S. al Coda

B7

You

CODA

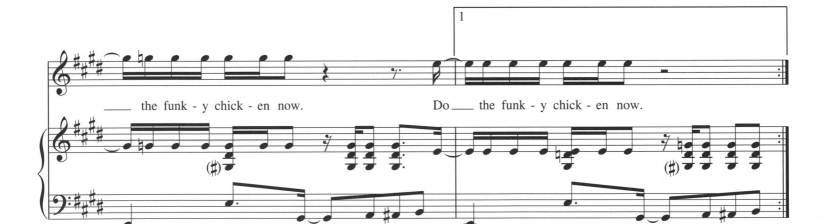

Do the funk - y chick - en now. Do ___ the funk - y chick - en now. Do ___

1

___ the funk - y chick - en now. Do ___ the funk - y chick - en now.

2

___ the funk - y chick - en now. Do ___ the funk - y chick - en now.

85

Play 4 times

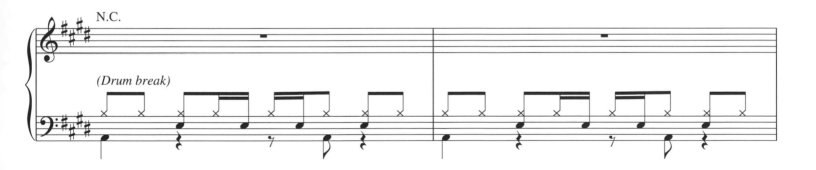

DOCTOR'S ORDERS

Words and Music by KIERAN KANE,
RORY MICHAEL BOURKE and BRUCE CHANNEL

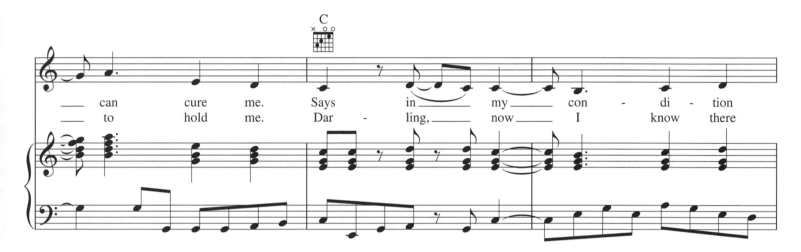

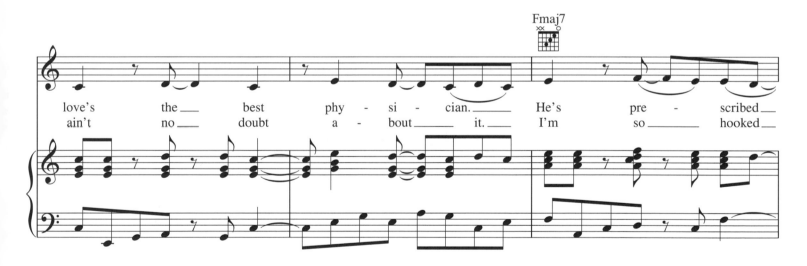

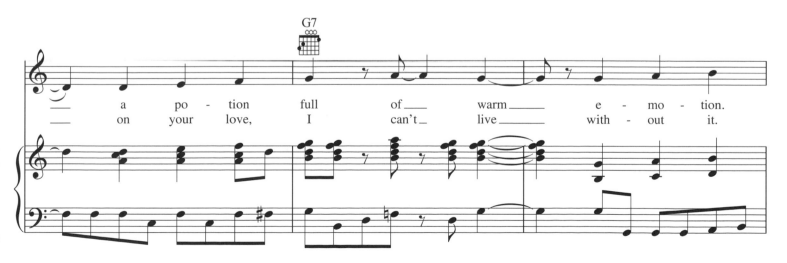

Ev - 'ry day _____ a lov - ing spoon - ful to be tak-
You're a - way, _____ but please don't treat _____ me like a stran-

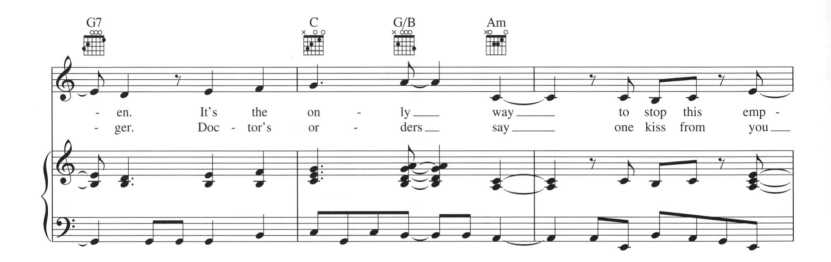

- en. It's the on - ly _____ way _____ to stop this emp -
- ger. Doc - tor's or - ders _____ say _____ one kiss from you _____

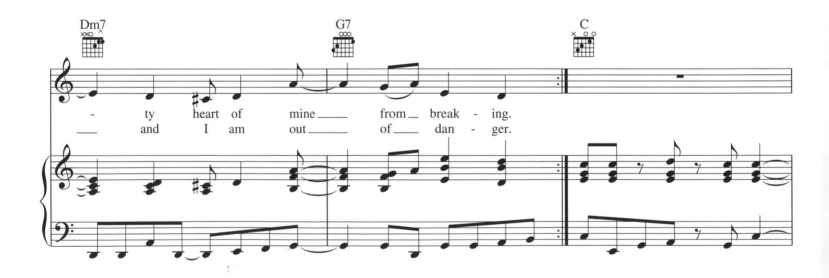

- ty heart of mine _____ from _ break - ing.
_____ and I am out _____ of _____ dan - ger.

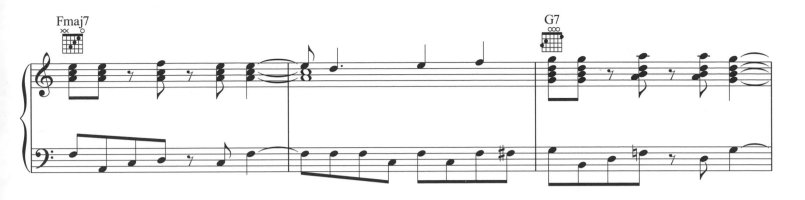

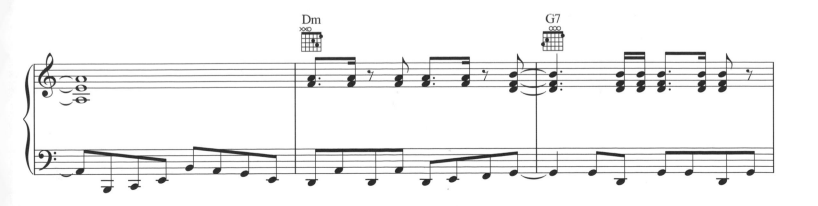

Spoken: *Please say you understand how I feel, honey.*

I know you've got a lot of things on your mind.

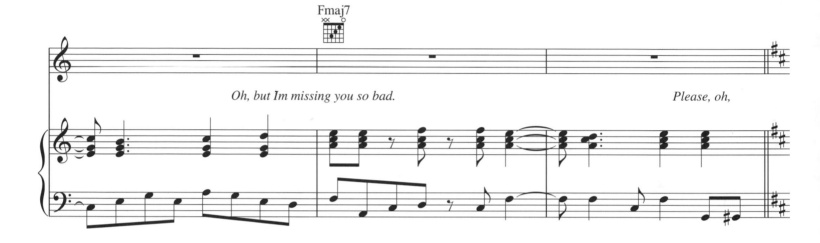

Oh, but Im missing you so bad.

Please, oh,

please, come on home.

(Hey, hey, hey, hey.)

Doc - tor's or -

- ders say there's on - ly one thing for me.

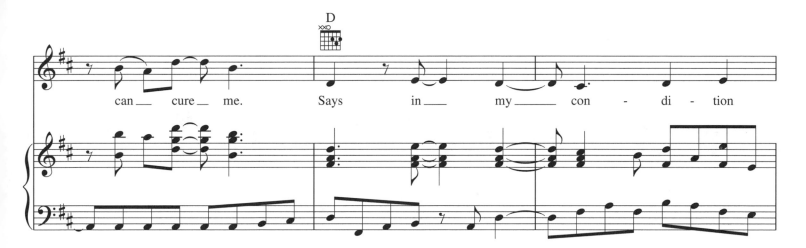

FIRE

Words and Music by RALPH MIDDLEBROOKS, MARSHALL JONES,
LEROY BONNER, CLARENCE SATCHELL,
WILLIE BECK and MARVIN PIERCE

got me burn-in', got me burn-in', got me burn-in', got me burn-

in'. Ooh ooh _____ ba-by,

a-burn-in', burn-in', ba-by. Ooh, _____

ooh,_ ooh,_ ooh, ___ burn-in', burn-in', ba-by.

FLASHDANCE...WHAT A FEELING
from the Paramount Picture FLASHDANCE

Lyrics by KEITH FORSEY and IRENE CARA
Music by GIORGIO MORODER

Steadily

First, when there's noth-ing but a slow glow-ing

dream, ____ that your fear seems to hide deep in-

side _____ your mind, All a-lone I have cried si-lent

FUNKYTOWN

Words and Music by
STEVEN GREENBERG

Moderately, with a beat

Got -

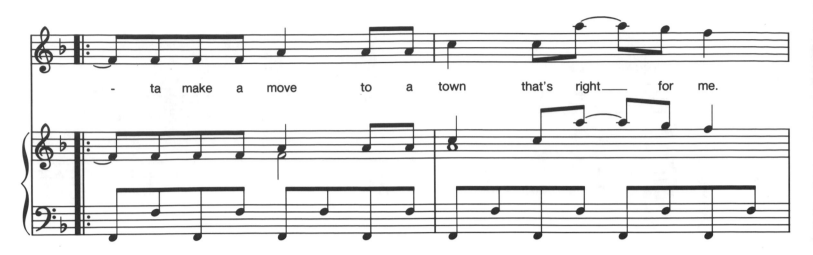

- ta make a move to a town that's right___ for me.

Town ___

___ to keep me mov - in', keep me groo - vin' with some en - er - gy. ___

___ Well, I

Got - ta move on.＿＿＿＿   Got - ta move on.＿＿＿＿

no chord

Fm7

Won't you take me to

(uh) funk - y - town.   Won't you take me to

(uh) funk - y - town.   Won't you take me to

(uh) funk - y - town.   Won't you take me to

F

(uh) funk - y - town.

Got -

funk - y - town.

GET DOWN TONIGHT

Words and Music by HARRY WAYNE CASEY
and RICHARD FINCH

Get down, get down, get down,_____ get down, get down to-night,___

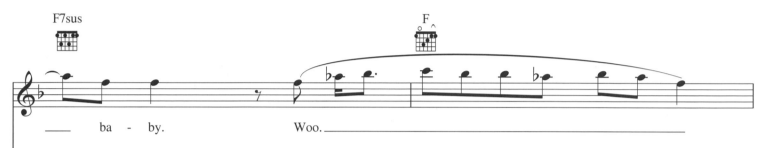

___ ba - by. Woo._____

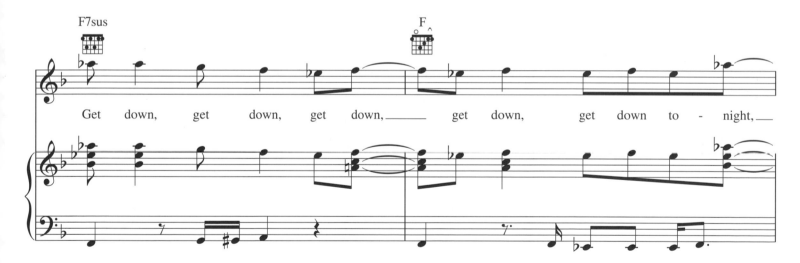

Get down, get down, get down,_____ get down, get down to-night,___

Repeat ad lib. and Fade

Optional Ending

___ ba - by. Na na na na na na na na na na. ___ ba - by.

8vb

GET UP (I FEEL LIKE BEING) A SEX MACHINE

Words and Music by JAMES BROWN, BOBBY BYRD
and RONALD LENHOFF

Shout: Fellas, I'm ready to get up and do my thing.
I wanta get into it, man, you know ...
Like a, like a sex machine, man,
Movin' ... doin' it, you know
Can I count it off? (Go ahead)

(E♭7)

use your form _ Stay on the scene like a

sex ma-chine. _ You got to have the feel - ing

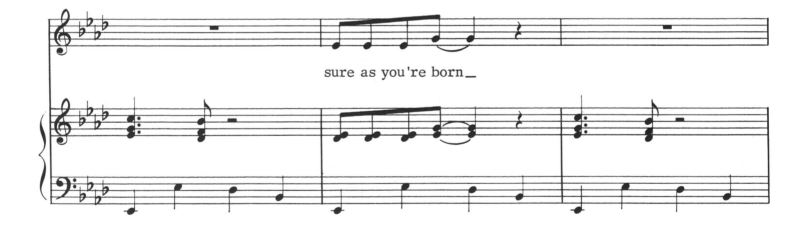

sure as you're born _

Get it to - geth - er right on, _ right on. _

ADDITIONAL WORDS

I said the feeling you got to get,
Give me the fever in a cold sweat.
The way I like it is the way it is;
I got mine and don't worry 'bout his.

Get on up and then shake your money maker,
Shake your money maker, etc.

GOOD TIMES

Words and Music by NILE RODGERS
and BERNARD EDWARDS

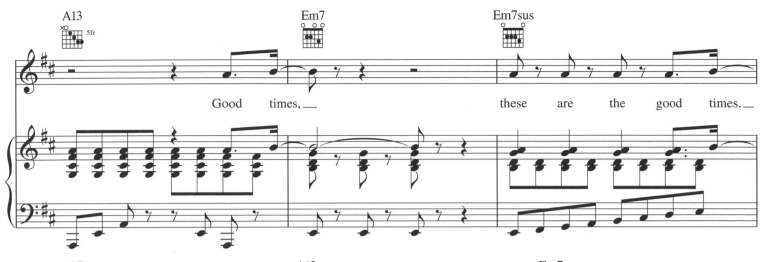

Good times, _____ these are the good times. ___

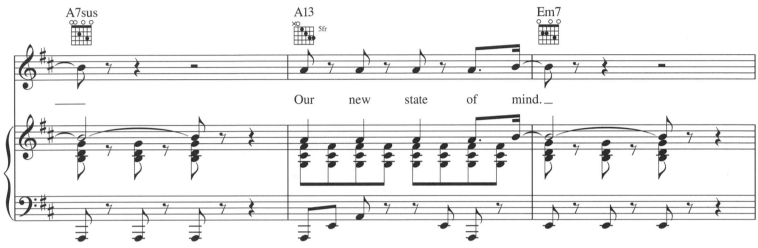

___ Our new state of mind. ___

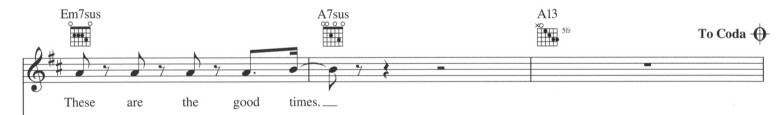

These are the good times. ___

To Coda ⊕

Hap - py days are here a - gain. The time is right for
A ru - mor has __ it that it's get - ting late. Time march - es on;

THE GROOVELINE

Words and Music by
ROD TEMPERTON

Moderately fast

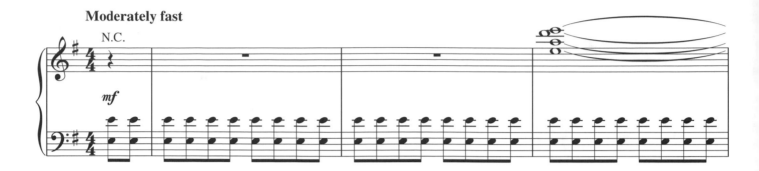

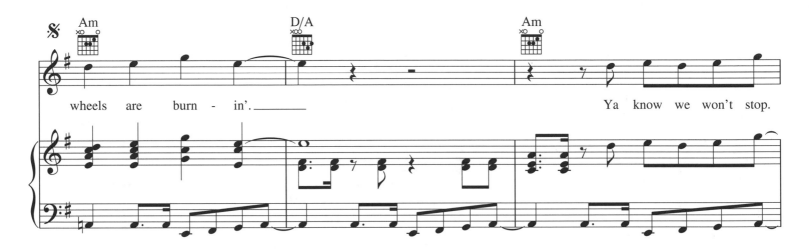

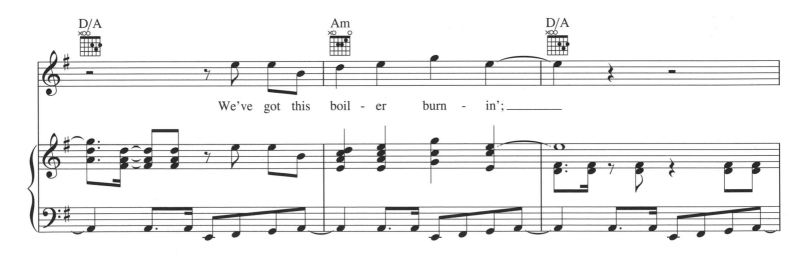

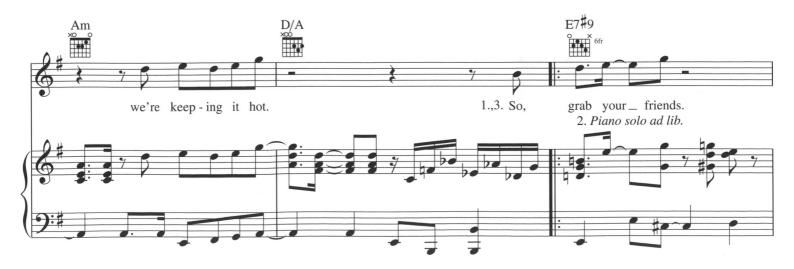

HARD TO HANDLE

Words and Music by ALLEN JONES,
ALVERTIS BELL and OTIS REDDING

Moderate Funk

1.,3. Ba - by, here I am ___ I'm a man on the scene. ___
2. *(See additional lyrics)*

I can give you what you want, _ but you got to go home _ with me.

I've got some good _ old lov - in' and I've got some in store. _

When I get _ through throw - in' it on _ you, you got to come back for more. ___

Boys and things will come _ by the doz-en; but that ain't noth - in' but drug-store lov-in'.

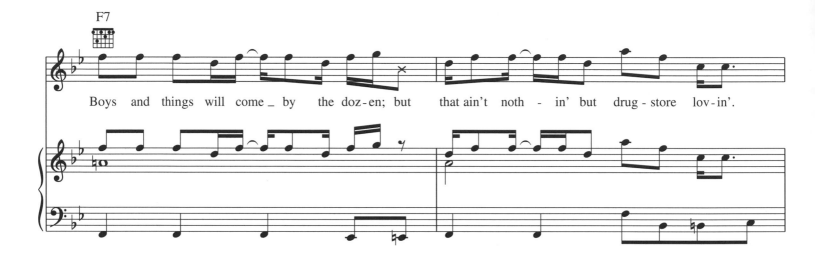

Pret-ty lit-tle thing, let me light the can - dle, 'cause ma-ma I'm sure _ hard to han-dle now, yes I am.

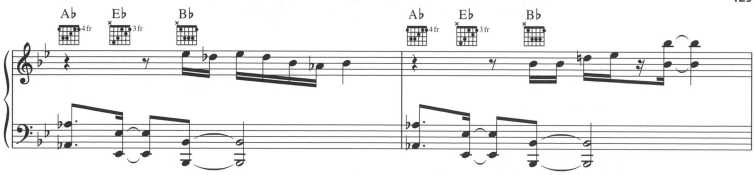

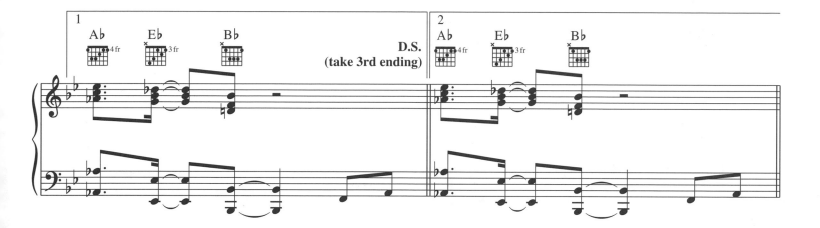

Additional Lyrics

2. Action speaks louder than words, and I'm a man with a great experience.
I know you got you another man, but I can love you better than him.
Take my hand, don't be afraid, I want to prove every word that I said.
I'm advertising love for free, so won't you place your ad with me?
Boys will come a dime by the dozen, but that ain't nothin' but kiss and look.
Pretty little thing, let me light the candle, 'cause mama, I'm sure hard to handle, now.

HEY POCKY WAY

Written by LEO NOCENTELLI, GEORGE PORTER,
JOSEPH MODELISTE and ARTHUR NEVILLE

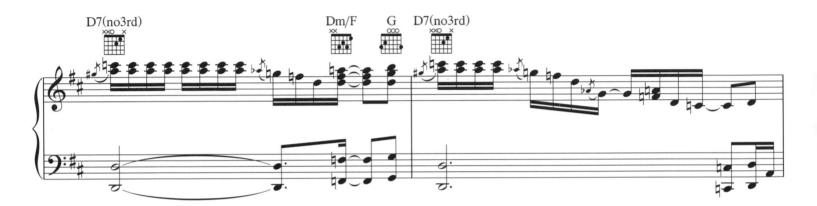

___ can't boog - ie now, but his sis - ter sure will, yeah. Feel -

__ good mu - sic, I've ___ been told, _____ is good ___

___ for your bod - y and it's good ___ for your soul. ___ { Move it to it, now. } { Come and get it, now. }

Hey, hey, hey, hey, hey pock - y way. ___

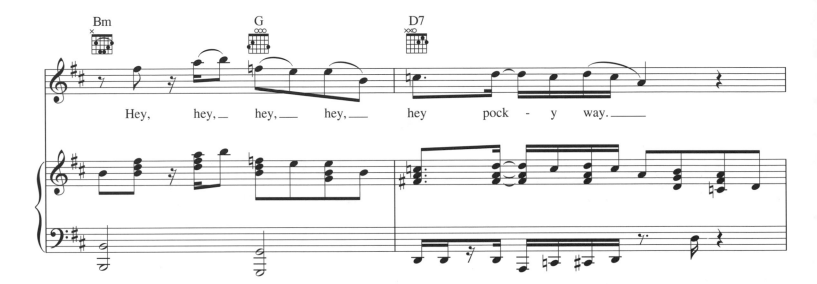

Hey, hey, ___ hey, ___ hey, ___ hey pock - y way. ___

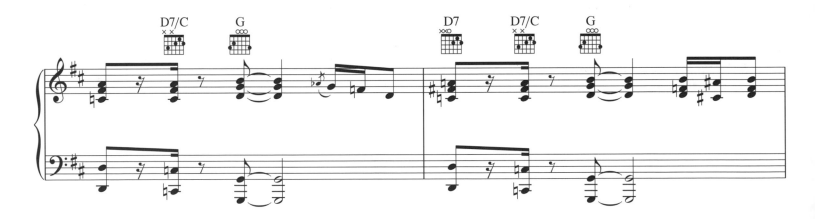

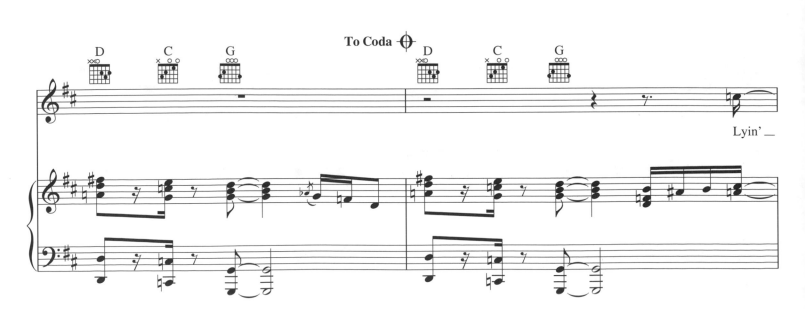

Lyin' ___

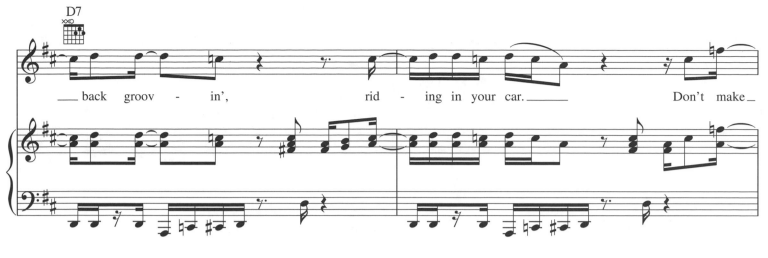

D7

_____ back groov - in', rid - ing in your car. _____ Don't make

_____ no dif - f'rence where _____ you are. _____ Feel -

- good mu - sic in _____ your soul _____ makes _____

_____ your bod - y do a slow _____ boog - ie roll. _____ Let me hear you say:

Hey, hey, hey, hey, hey pock - y way.____

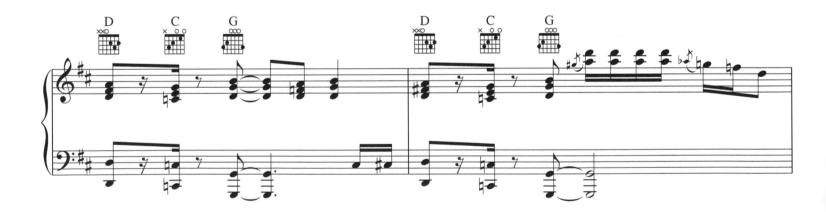

Hey, hey,___ hey,___ hey,_____ hey pock - y way.____

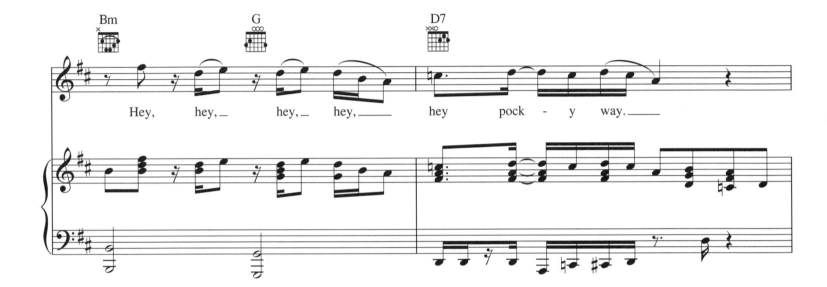

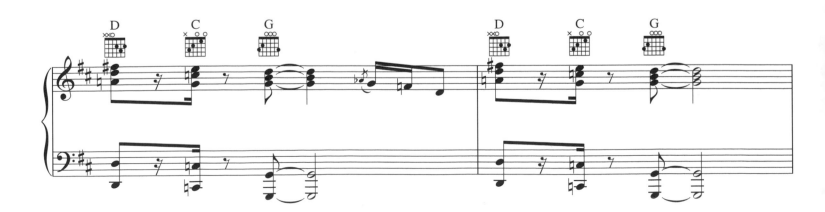

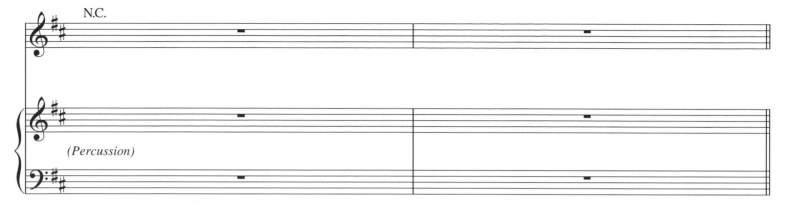

N.C.

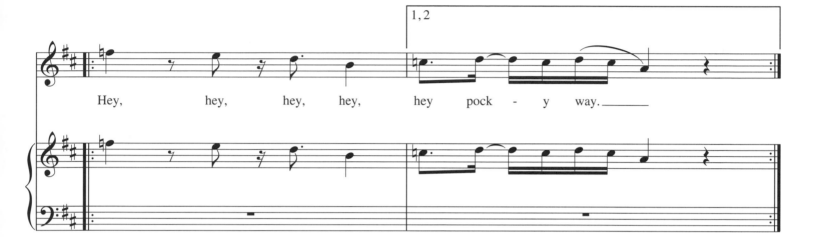

(Percussion)

1, 2

Hey,   hey,   hey,   hey,   hey pock - y way._____

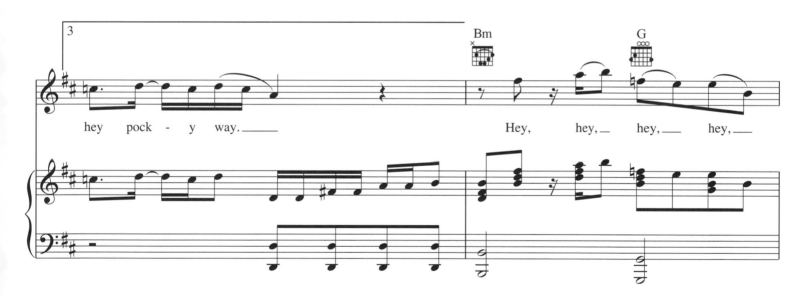

3

hey pock - y way._____   Bm   G   Hey,   hey,___ hey,___ hey,___

D7

hey   pock - y   way._____

Keep on groov - in', y'all. Keep on get - tin' down. Keep

on get - tin' on and down.

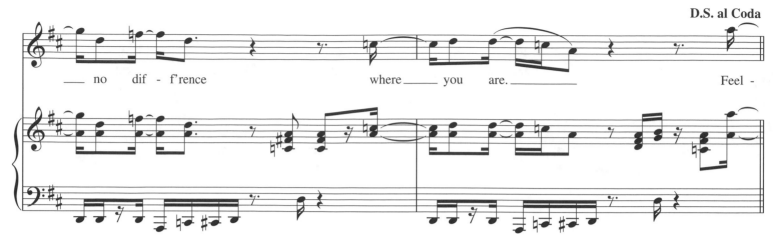

no dif - f'rence where you are. Feel -

Hey pock - y way.

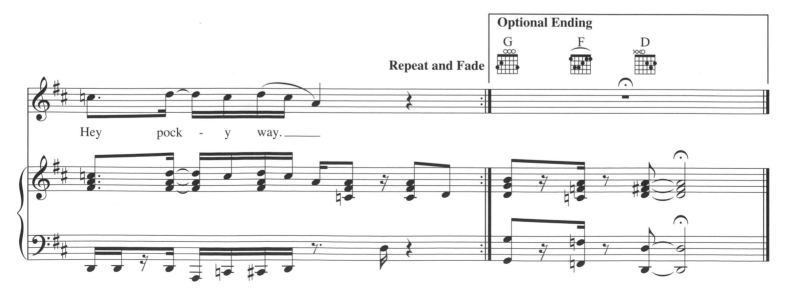

Hey pock - y way.

HOT STUFF

Words and Music by PETE BELLOTTE,
HAROLD FALTERMEYER and KEITH FORSEY

HIGHER GROUND

Words and Music by
STEVIE WONDER

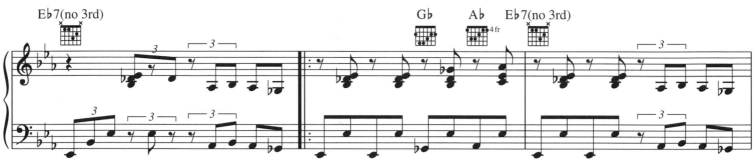

Peo - ple, ___
Pow - ers, ___
Lov - ers, ___

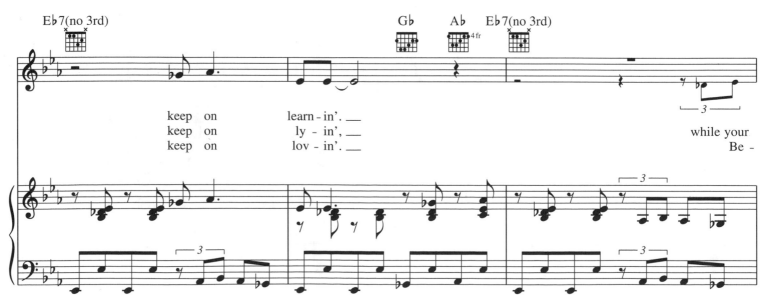

keep on learn - in'. ___
keep on ly - in', ___
keep on lov - in'. ___

while your
Be -

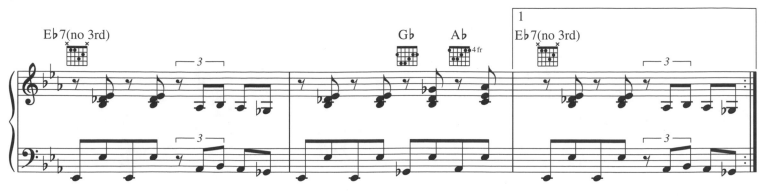

I'm so { darn glad / glad that } he let me try it a - gain, _ 'cause my

last time on earth I lived a whole world of sin. _ I'm so glad that I know _ more

than I knew then. _ Gon - na keep _ on try - in', till _ I reach _ { the / my } high - est

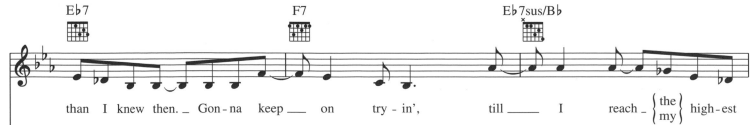

HOW DEEP IS YOUR LOVE

from the Motion Picture SATURDAY NIGHT FEVER

Words and Music by BARRY GIBB,
MAURICE GIBB and ROBIN GIBB

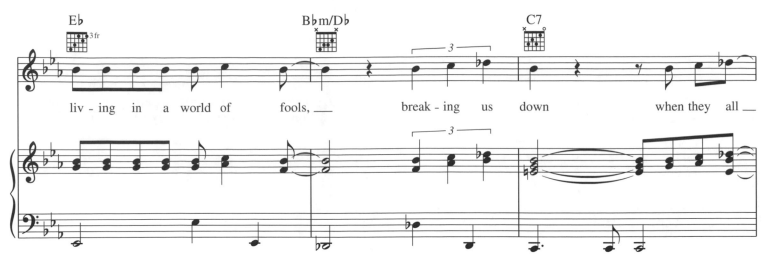

living in a world of fools, ___ break-ing us down when they all ___

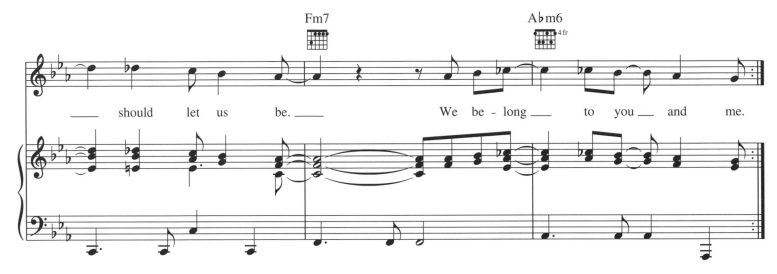

___ should let us be. ___ We be-long ___ to you ___ and me.

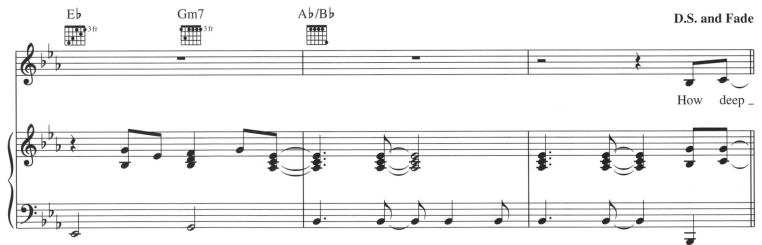

D.S. and Fade

How deep ___

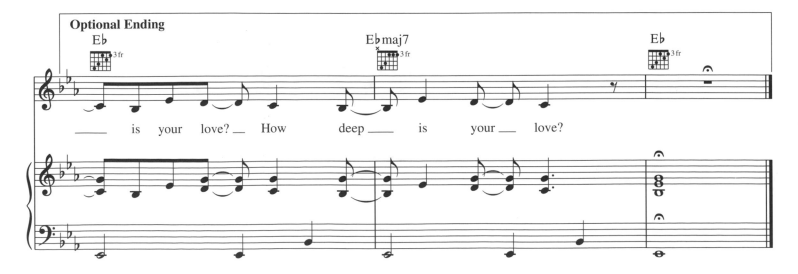

Optional Ending

___ is your love? ___ How deep ___ is your ___ love?

I GOT THE FEELIN'

Words and Music by
JAMES BROWN

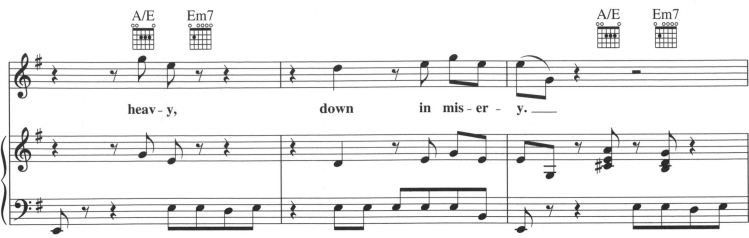

heav - y, down in mis - er - y. ___

Hey, yeah, ___ *(Spoken:)* al - right, ow!

Hey, hey, *(Sung:)* ah. _____

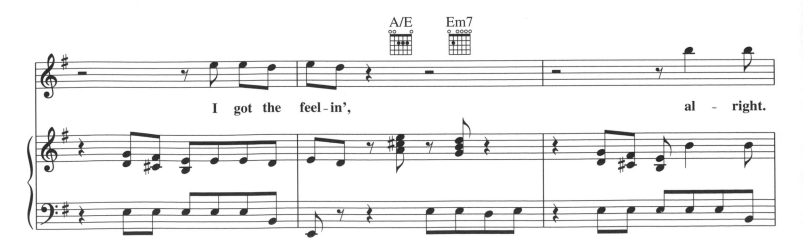

I got the feel - in', al - right.

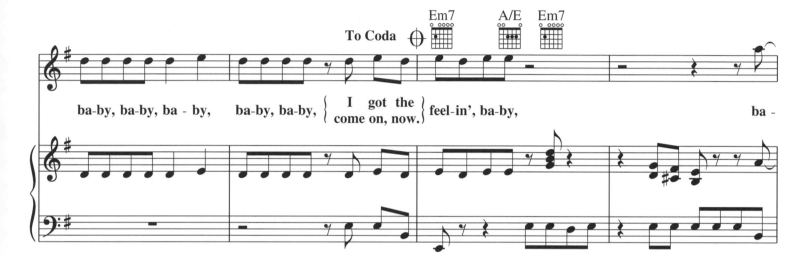

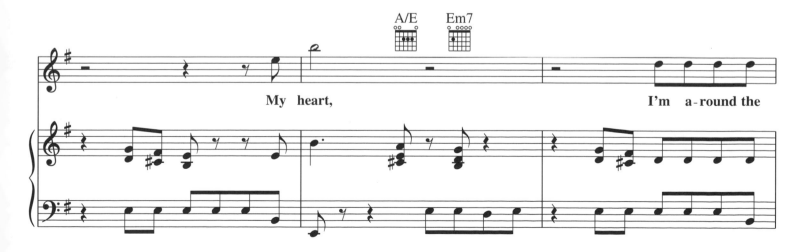

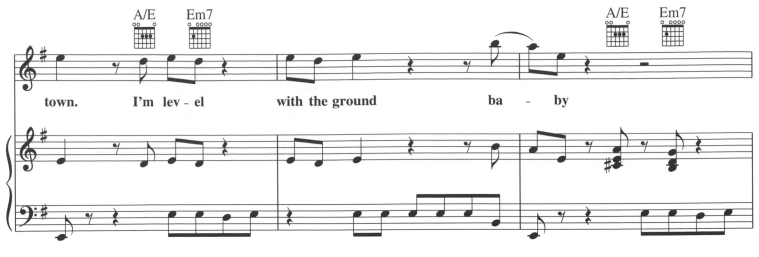

town.   I'm lev - el   with the ground   ba - by

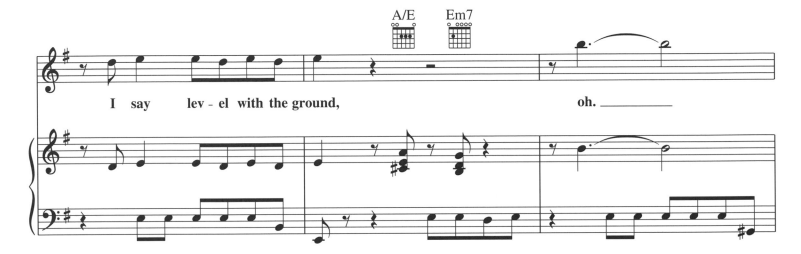

I say   lev - el with the ground,   oh. _____

No,   I know,   no, you don't

mean it now. Some-times I roam, _

but I'll be com-in' back home. _ Some-times I

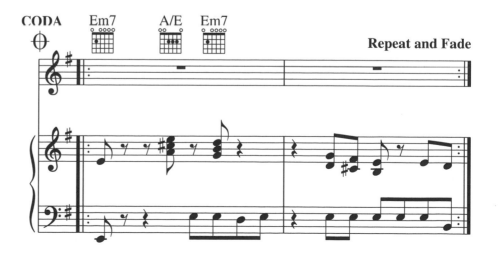

seem to be fly; _ I just don't know when to say bye-bye,

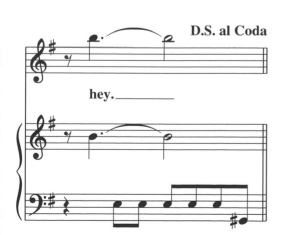

D.S. al Coda

hey. _

CODA   Em7   A/E   Em7

Repeat and Fade

I JUST WANT TO BE YOUR EVERYTHING

Words and Music by
BARRY GIBB

I JUST WANT TO CELEBRATE

Words and Music by NICK ZESSES
and DINO FEKARIS

Moderately

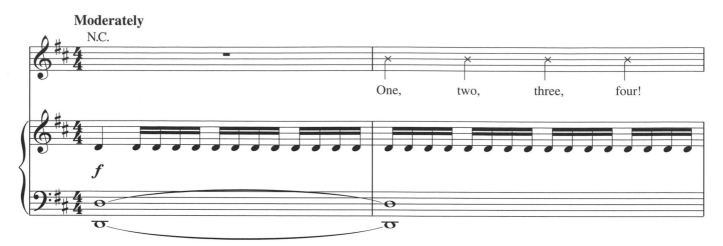

One, two, three, four!

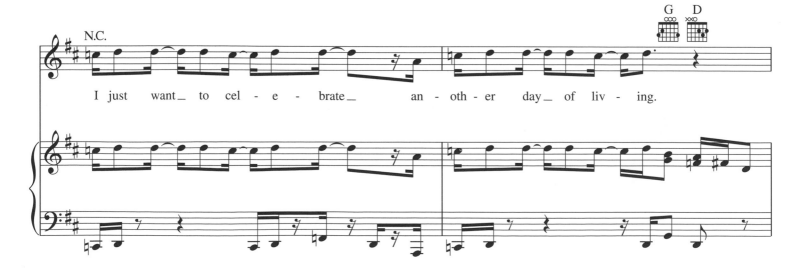

I just want_ to cel - e - brate_ an - oth - er day_ of liv - ing.

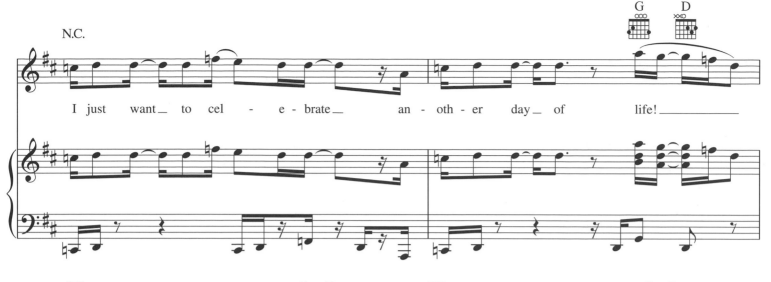

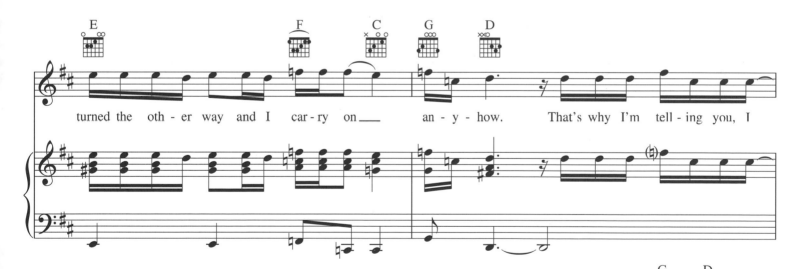

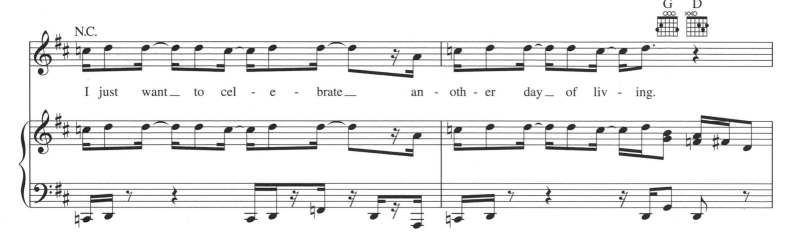

I just want to cel - e - brate an - oth - er day of liv - ing.

I just want to cel - e - brate an - oth - er day of

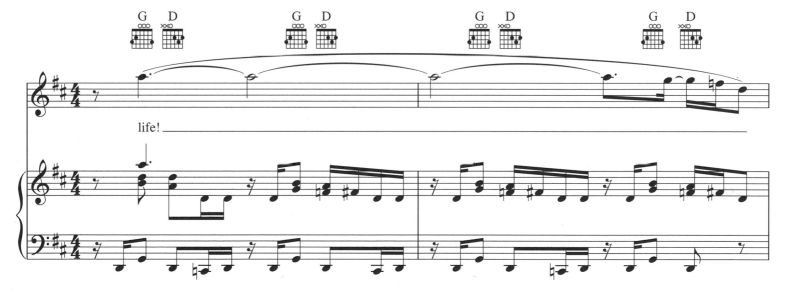

life! _____

Don't let it all get you down no, no. Don't let it turn you a -

round and a - round and a - round and a - round and a - round and a - round.

Guitar solo ad lib.

Well, I can't be both - ered with sor - row, and I

can't be both - ered with hate. __ I'm us - ing up my time by feel - ing fine __

ev - 'ry day. That's why I'm tell - ing you, I just want to cel - e - brate.

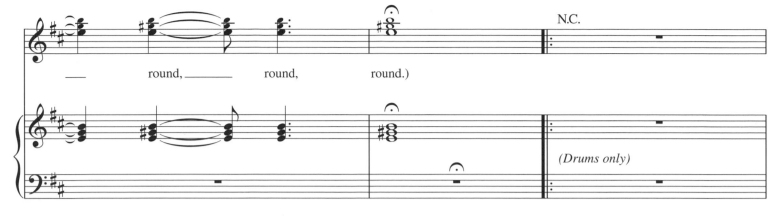

round, round, round.)

N.C.

(Drums only)

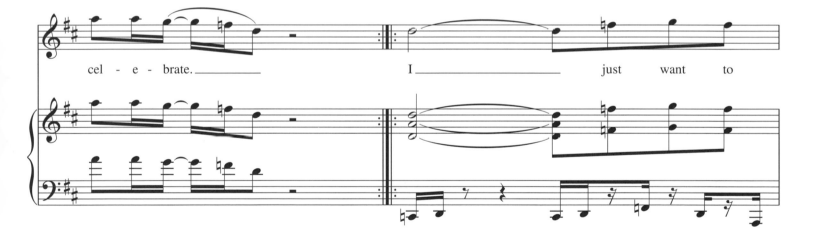

I _____ just want to

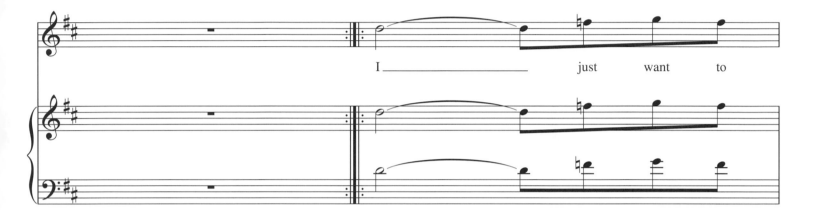

cel - e - brate. _____ I _____ just want to

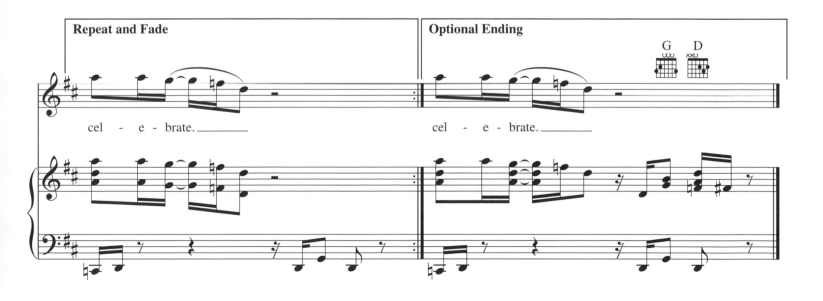

Repeat and Fade

cel - e - brate. _____

Optional Ending

cel - e - brate. _____

G   D

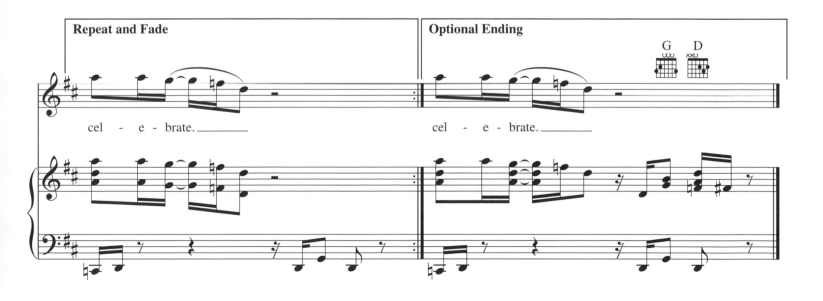

I LOVE THE NIGHT LIFE

Words and Music by ALICIA BRIDGES
and SUSAN HUTCHESON

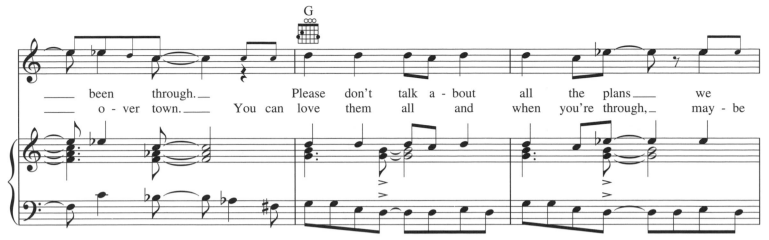

been through.____ Please don't talk a - bout all the plans____ we
o - ver town.____ You can love them all and when you're through,_ may - be

had____ for fix - in' this bro - ken ro - mance.____
that -'ll make a man out of you.____

I want to go where the

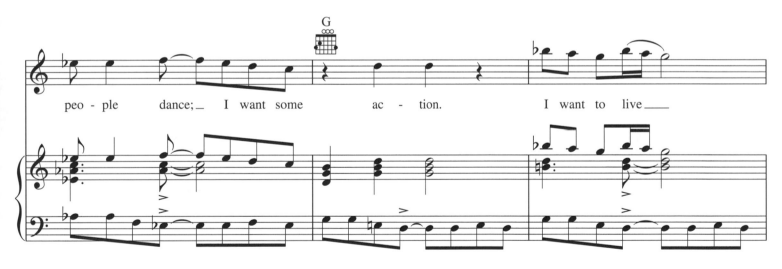

peo - ple dance;_ I want some ac - tion. I want to live____

ac - tion. I've got so much to give.____ I want to give it,

I WANT YOU BACK

Words and Music by FREDDIE PERREN, ALPHONSO MIZELL,
BERRY GORDY and DEKE RICHARDS

When I had _ you to _ my - self, _ I did-n't want you a - round. _ Those
Try-ing to live with - out _ your love _ is one long sleep-less night. _

pret - ty fac - es al - ways made _ you stand out in a crowd. _ Then
Let me show _ you, girl, _____ that I know wrong from right. _____

some - one picked you from _ the bunch, _ one glance was all it took. _
Ev - 'ry street you walk _ on, I _____ leave tear - stains on the ground, _

IF I CAN'T HAVE YOU

Words and Music by BARRY GIBB,
MAURICE GIBB and ROBIN GIBB

LADY MARMALADE

Words and Music by BOB CREWE
and KENNY NOLAN

Moderate groove

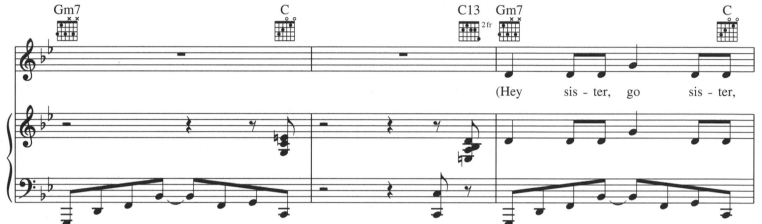

(Hey sis-ter, go sis-ter,

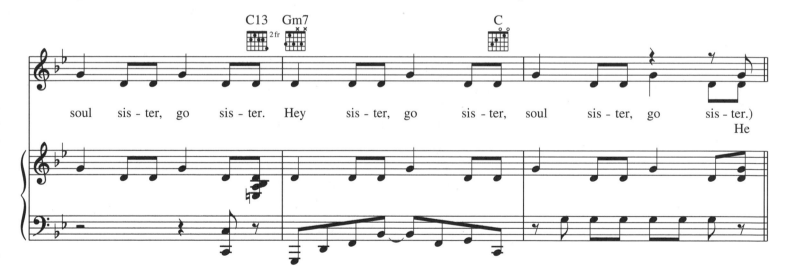

soul sis-ter, go sis-ter. Hey sis-ter, go sis-ter, soul sis-ter, go sis-ter.) He

met Mar-ma-lade down in old New Or-leans, strut-tin' her stuff on the street.

She said, __ "Hel-lo, hey Joe, you wan-na

give it a go?" __ Mm hmm. Get-cha get-cha ya ya da __

__ da. Get-cha get-cha ya ya here. __

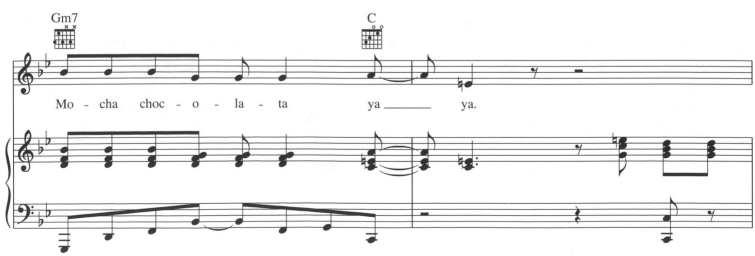

Mo - cha choc - o - la - ta ya _____ ya.

Cm7   G5

cues 1st time only

To Coda ⊕

Cre - ole La - dy Mar - ma - lade. ___

Gm7   C   Gm7   C

Vou - lez vous cou - cher a - vec moi ___ ce soir?   Vou - lez vous cou - cher a - vec moi? ___

1

Gm7   C

___ Stayed in her bou - doir while she ___ fresh-ened up; ___
(Hey sis - ter, go sis - ter, soul sis - ter, go sis - ter.

Gm7   C

that boy drank all that mag - no - lia wine.   On her
Hey sis - ter, go sis - ter, soul sis - ter, go sis - ter.)

black sat - in sheets, I swear __ he start-ed to freak. __ __

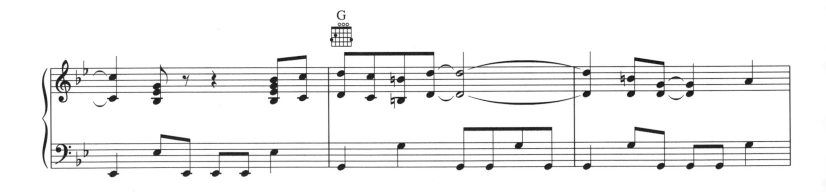

Hey, __ hey, __ hey __

hey - ey - ey. ____ Seein' her skin, __ feel - ing silk - y smooth,

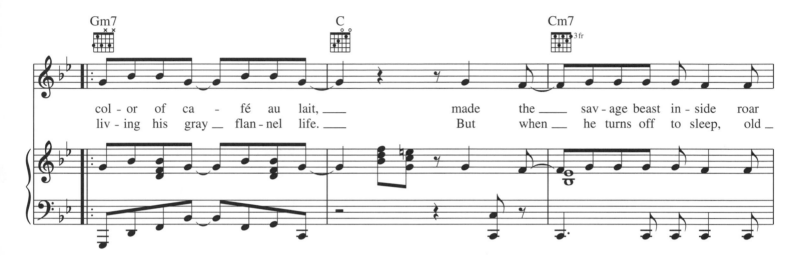

col - or of ca - fé au lait, ____ made the ____ sav - age beast in - side roar

liv - ing his gray ___ flan - nel life. ____ But when __ he turns off to sleep, old __

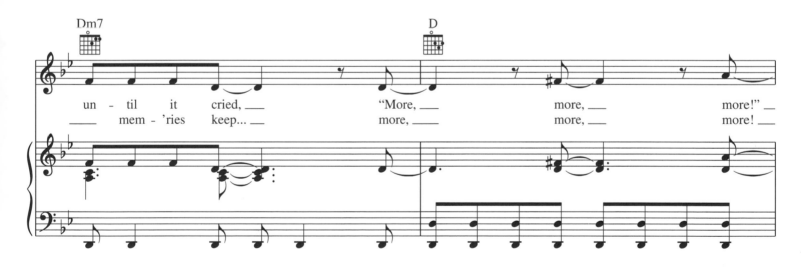

un - til it cried, ___ "More, ___ more, ___ more!" __

__ mem - 'ries keep... __ more, ___ more, ___ more! __

Now he's at home _ do - ing nine - to - five,

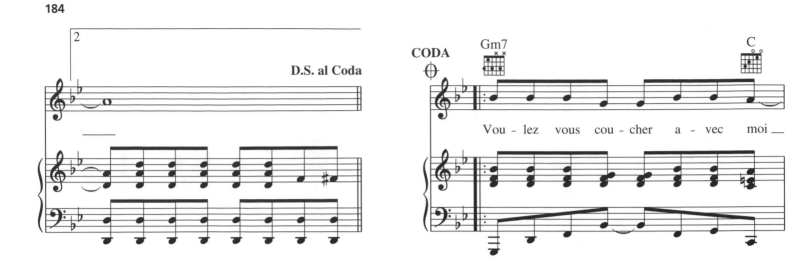

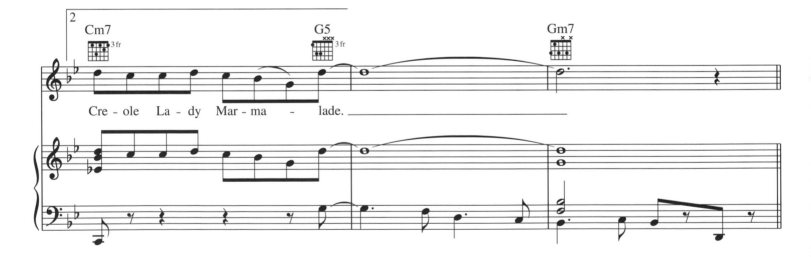

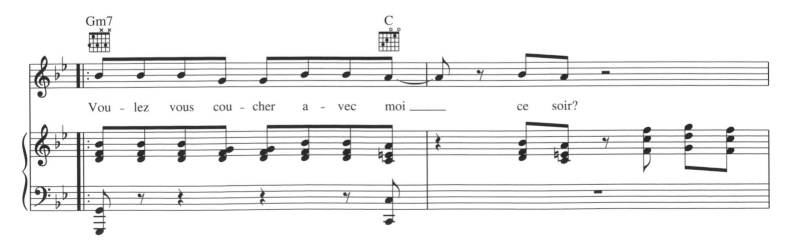

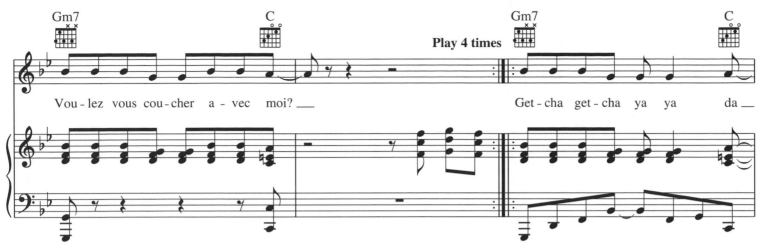

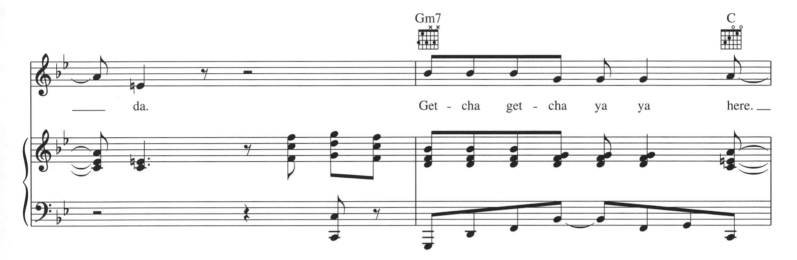

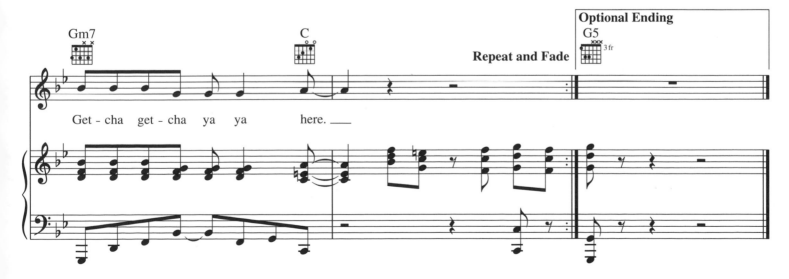

IN THE NAVY

Words and Music by JACQUES MORALI,
HENRI BELOLO and VICTOR WILLIS

Steady Disco beat

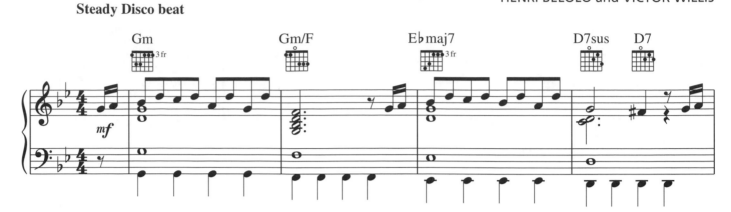

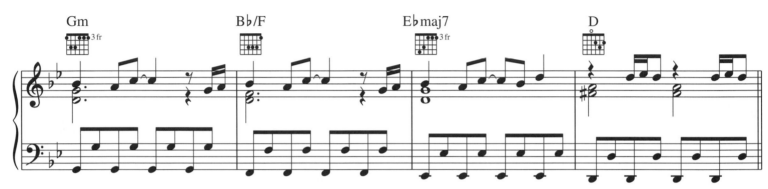

1. Where can you find pleas - ure, search ___ the world for treas - ure,
2. Where can you learn to fly, play ___ in sports or skin dive,
3. *(See additional lyrics)*

learn sci - ence tech - nol - o - gy? ___
stud - y o - cean - og - ra - phy? ___

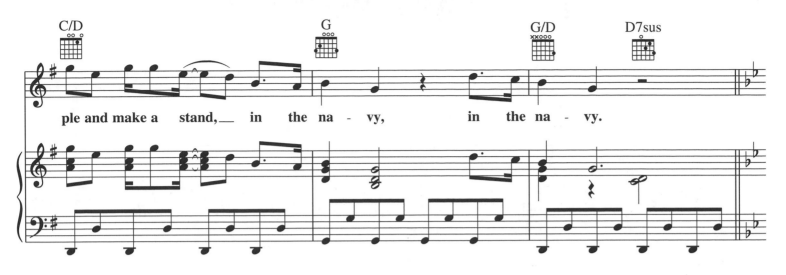

ple and make a stand,__ in the na - vy, in the na - vy.

(hand claps)

(Shout:) They want you! They want you!

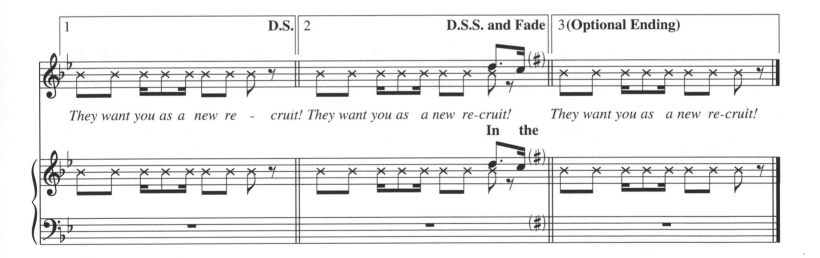

1 **D.S.** **2** **D.S.S. and Fade** **3** **(Optional Ending)**

They want you as a new re - cruit! They want you as a new re-cruit! They want you as a new re-cruit!

In the

Additional Lyrics

3. If you like adventure,
   Don't you wait to enter
   The recruiting office fast.
   Don't you hesitate,
   There is no need to wait;
   They're signing up new seamen fast.
   Maybe you are too young to join up today,
   But don't you worry 'bout a thing,
   For I'm sure there will be always
   The good navy protecting the land and sea.
   To Chorus:

IT'S RAINING MEN

Words and Music by PAUL JABARA
and PAUL SHAFFER

Moderate Dance

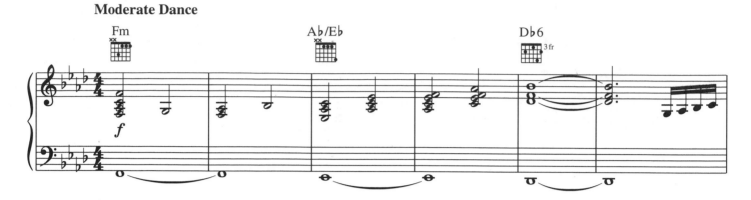

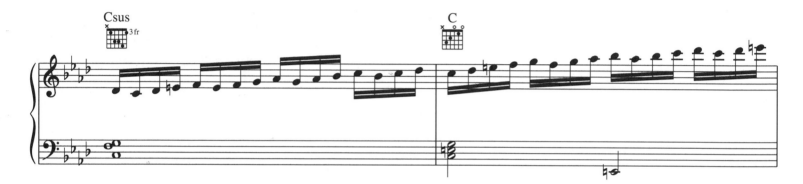

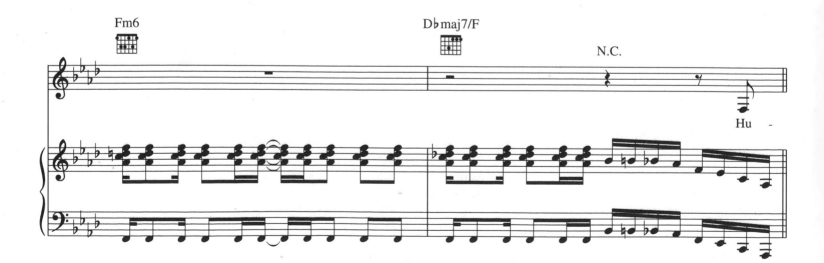

Hu -

mid - i - ty's ris - ing. ____ Ba -

rom - e - ter's get - ting low. _____ Ac -

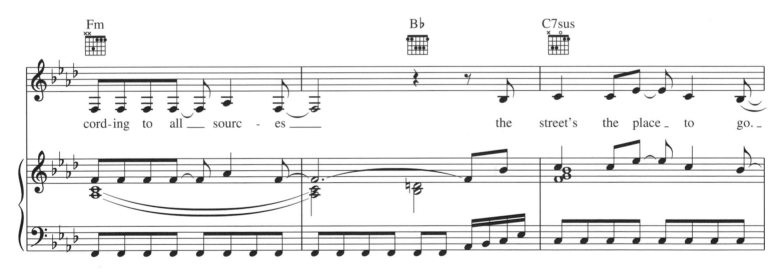

cord - ing to all ___ sourc - es ____ the street's the place __ to go. __

_____ 'Cause to - night for the first ___ time ___ at

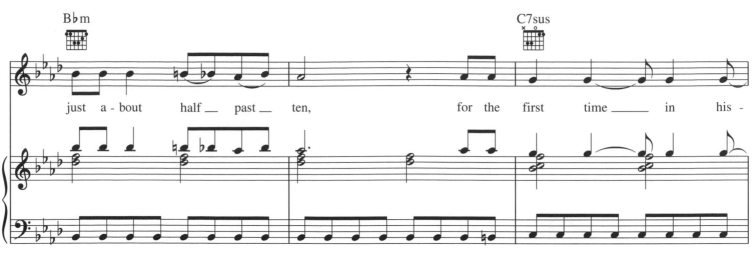

just a-bout half __ past __ ten, for the first time __ in his-

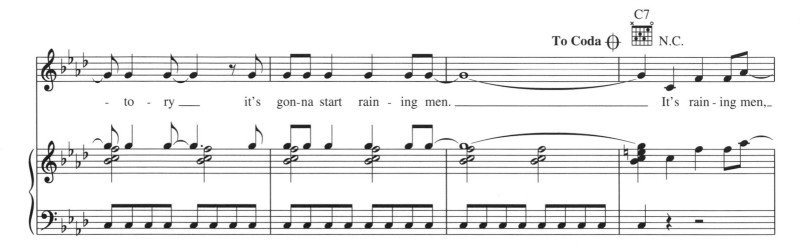

-to-ry __ it's gon-na start rain-ing men. __ It's rain-ing men, __

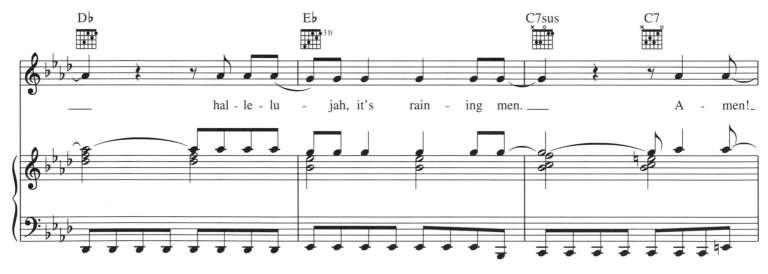

__ hal-le-lu - jah, it's rain - ing men. __ A - men!

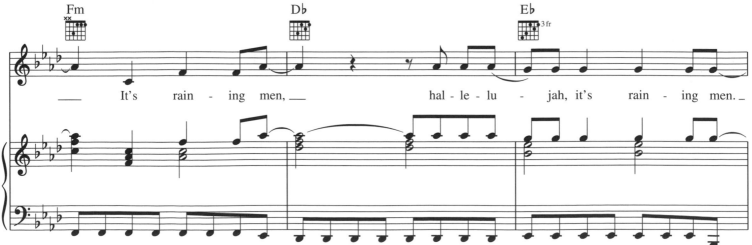

__ It's rain - ing men, __ hal-le-lu - jah, it's rain - ing men. __

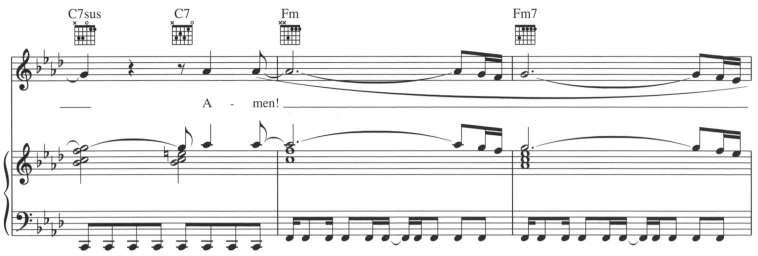

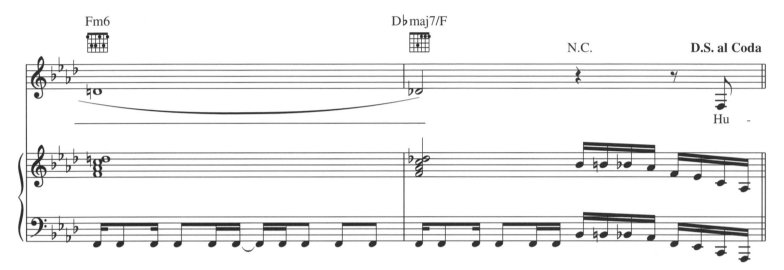

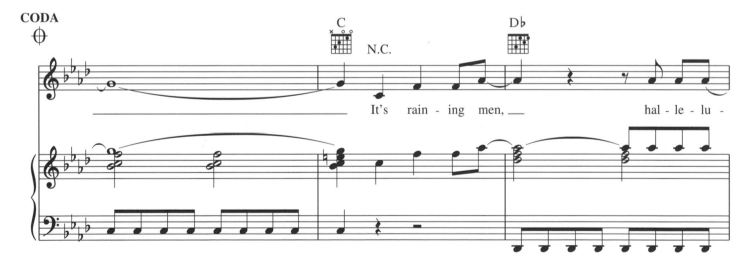

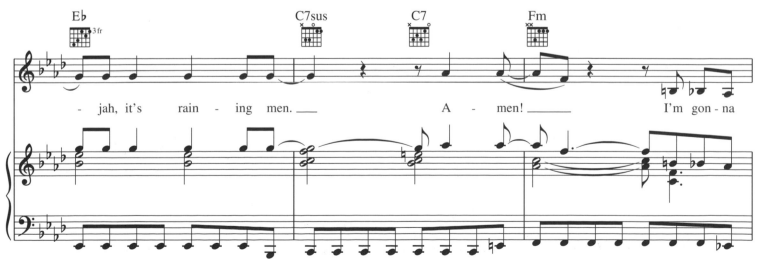

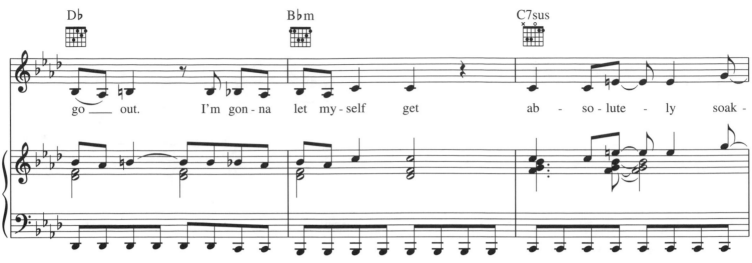

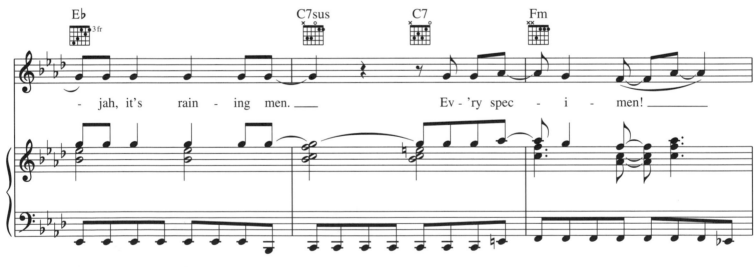

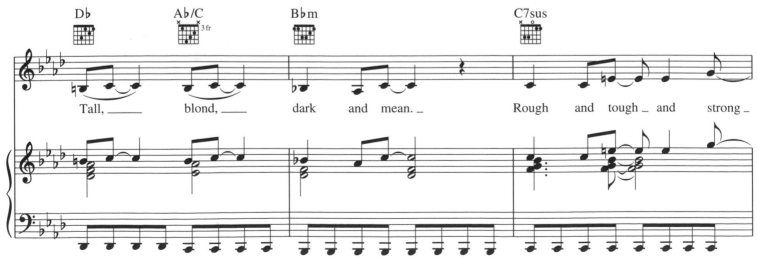

195

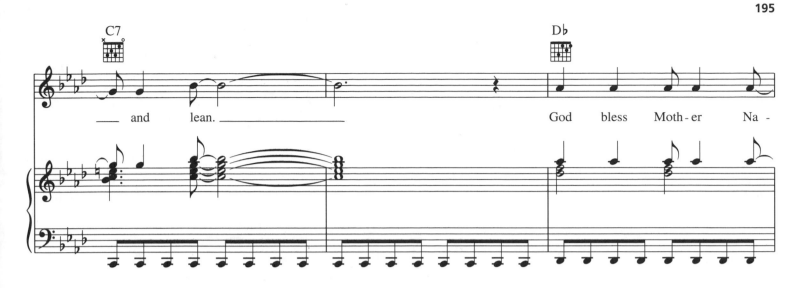

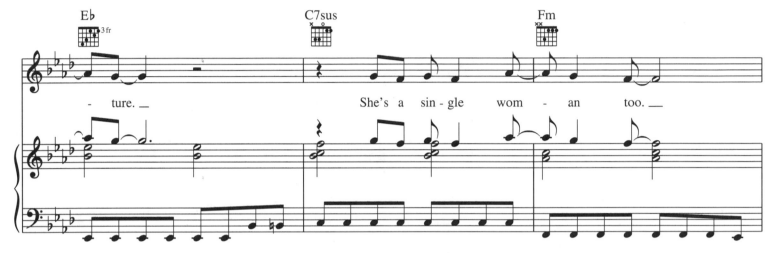

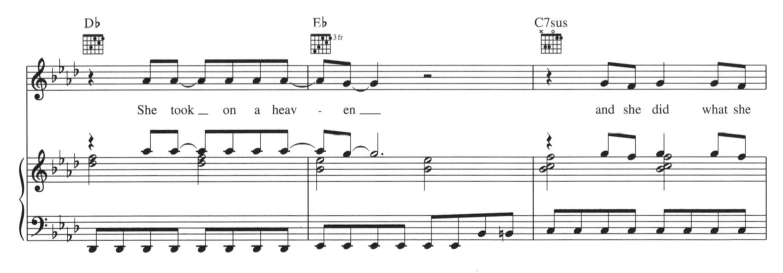

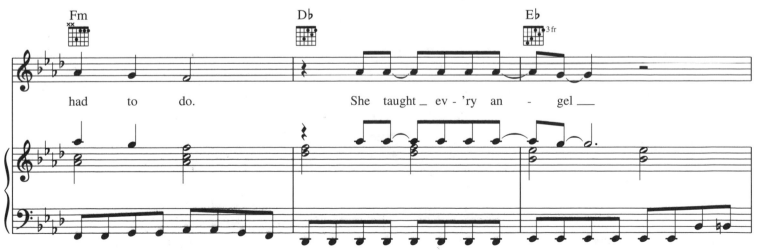

to re-ar-range the sky ___ so that each and ev-'ry wom-

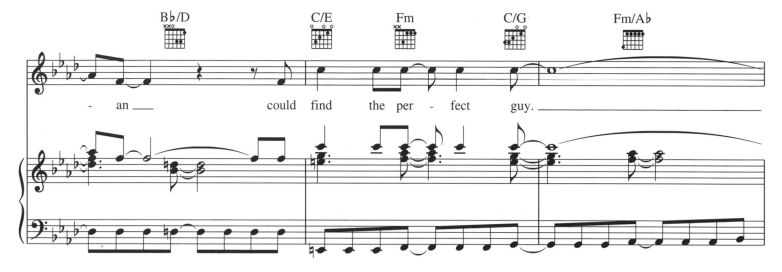

-an ___ could find the per-fect guy. ___

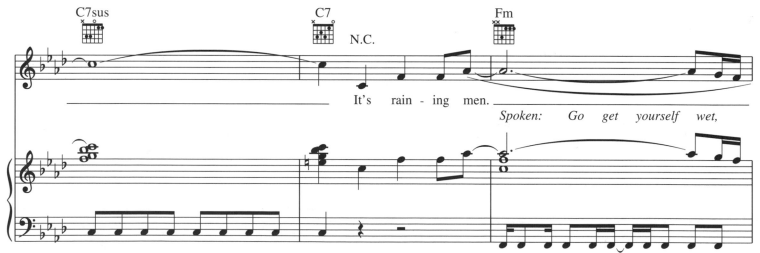

___ It's rain-ing men. ___

Spoken: Go get yourself wet,

girl! *I know you want to.*

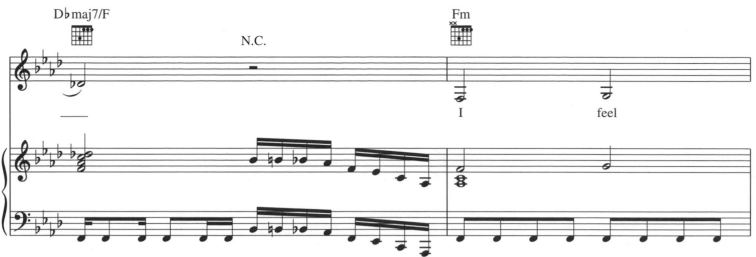

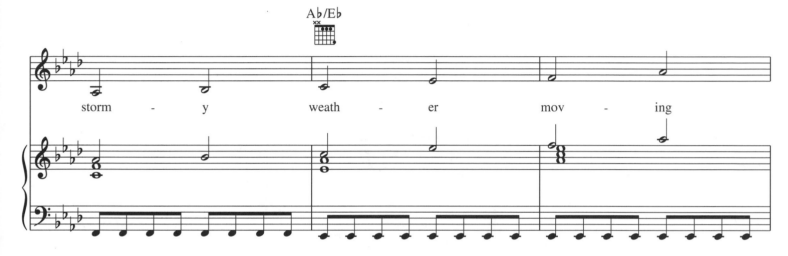

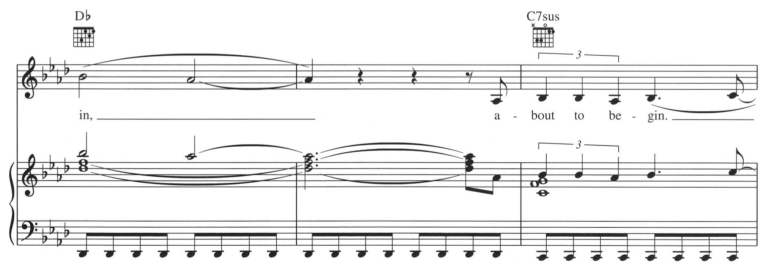

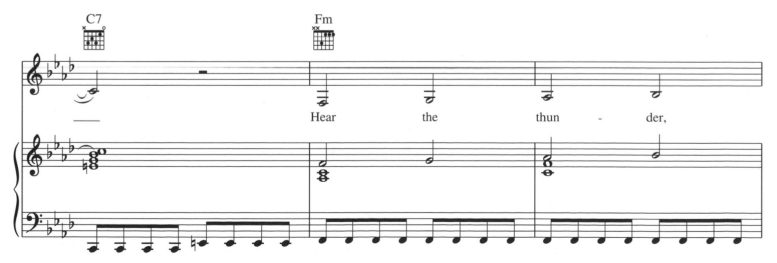

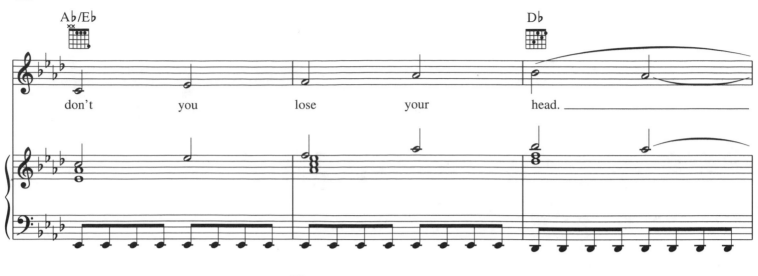

don't you lose your head. _____

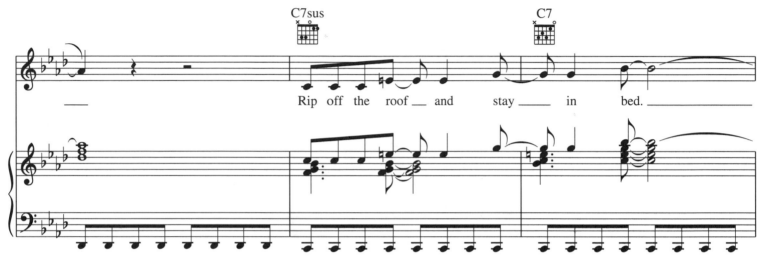

_____ Rip off the roof ___ and stay ___ in bed. _____

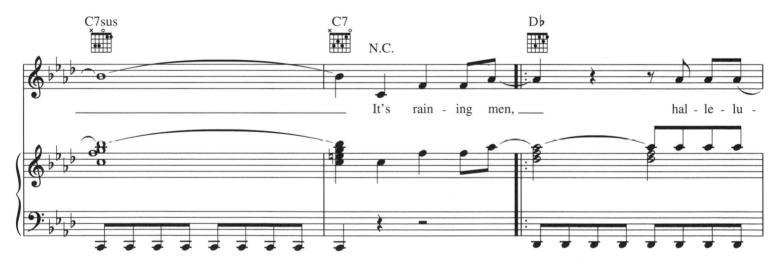

_____ It's rain - ing men, ___ hal - le - lu -

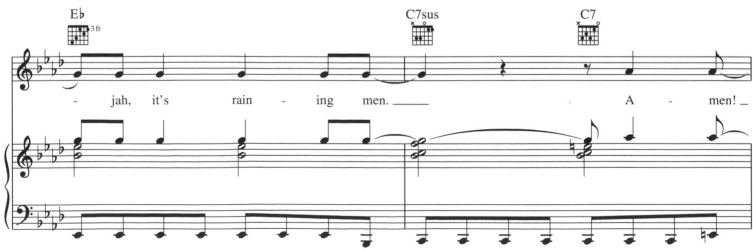

- jah, it's rain - ing men. _____ A - men! _

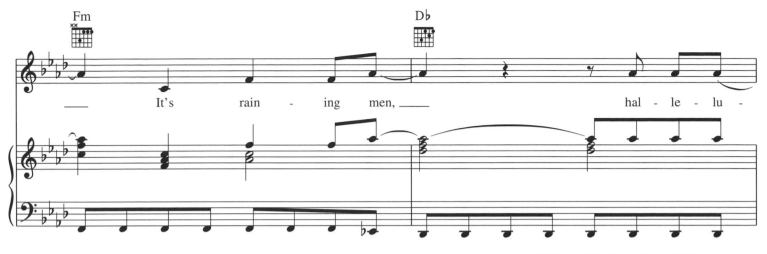

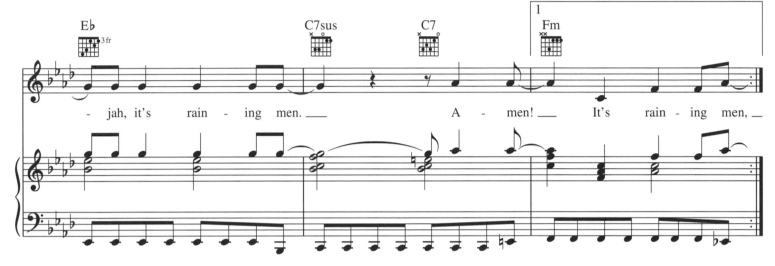

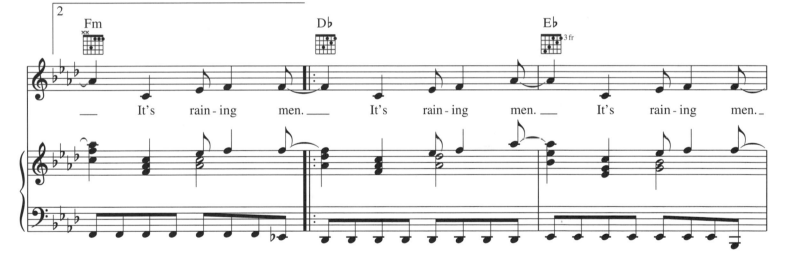

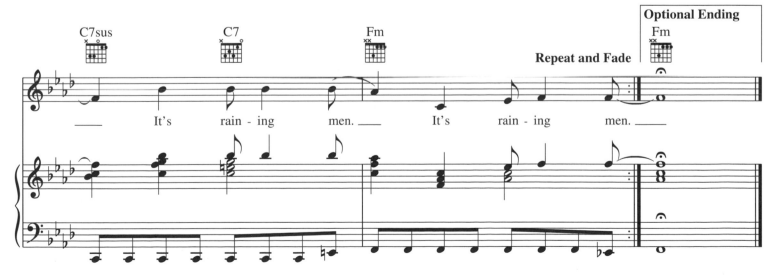

IT'S YOUR THING

Words and Music by RUDOLPH ISLEY, RONALD ISLEY
and O'KELLY ISLEY

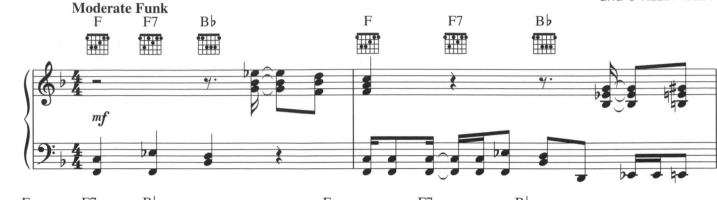

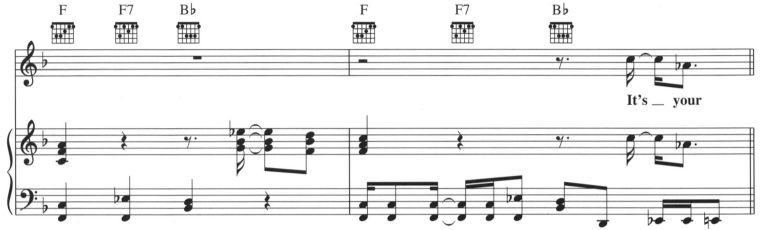

thing,   do what you wan-na do. __   I can't tell you,   who to

sock it to. __

{ If you want   me to love ya',   may-be __ I   will. __
  I'm   not   try - in'   to   run your   life. __

Be - lieve __ me wom - an,   it ain't   no big   deal. __
I   know you   wan - na   do what's   right. __

Oh,   you need   love __ now   just as bad __ as I
Oh,   give your love __ girl,   do what-ev - er you

JIVE TALKIN'
from SATURDAY NIGHT FEVER

Words and Music by BARRY GIBB,
MAURICE GIBB and ROBIN GIBB

Moderately, with a strong beat

Tacet

It's just your jive talk-in', you're tell-in' me lies,__ yeah; jive talk-in', you wear a dis-guise.__ Jive talk-in', so mis-un-der-stood,__ yeah; jive talk-in', you're

gets in my eyes.__ No - bod - y be - lieves what you say; __ it's just your
wear a dis - guise.__ Jive talk - in', so mis - un - der - stood,_ yeah;

jive talk - in' that gets in the way.__ Love talk - in' is
jive talk - in', you just ain't no good.__

all ver - y fine,_ yeah; jive talk - in' just is - n't a crime.__ And if there's

some - bod - y you'll love till you die, __ then all that jive talk - in' just

LE FREAK

Words and Music by NILE RODGERS
and BERNARD EDWARDS

LOVE IS THICKER THAN WATER

Words and Music by BARRY GIBB
and ANDY GIBB

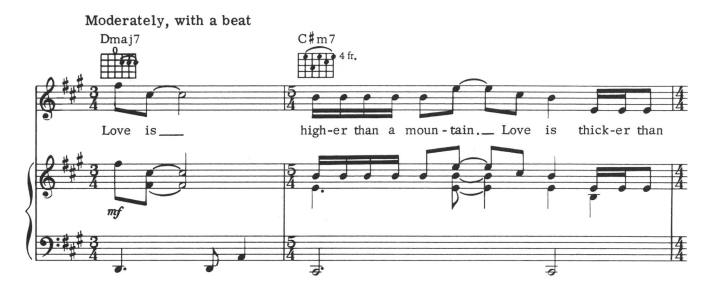

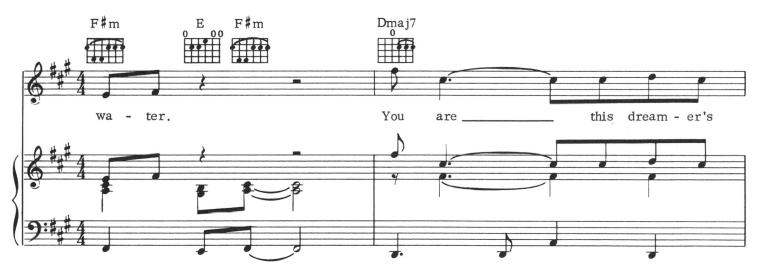

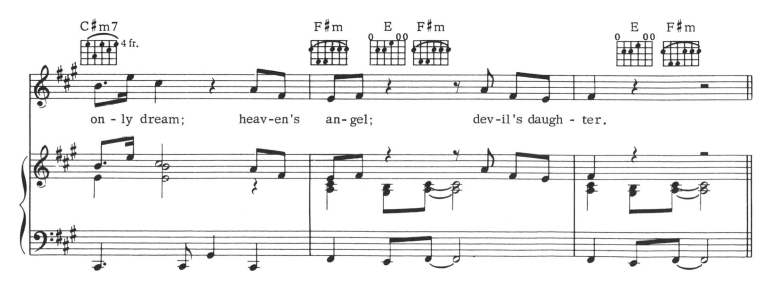

LET'S GROOVE

Words and Music by MAURICE WHITE
and WAYNE VAUGHN

Dm7　　Gm7　　　　　F#m7♭5　　　　　　　B7#9

_ if you want my love _ we can boo - gie on

no chord　　　　　　　　　　　　(Play 3 times)

down,　　　　down.　Boo - gie on　down,　on

Em7　　　　Em7/A　　　F#m7　　Bm7

down,　　boo - gie. Let's　groove to - night,　　　　share the

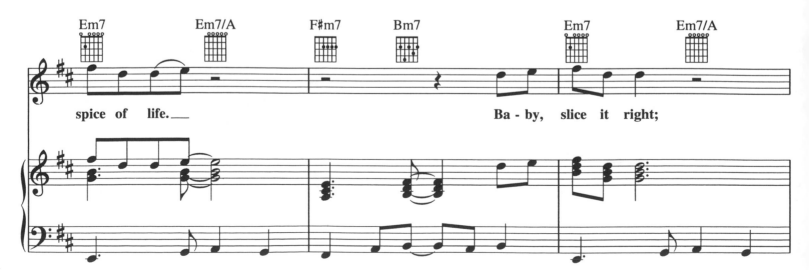

Em7　　　Em7/A　　　F#m7　　Bm7　　　　Em7　　　Em7/A

spice of life. _　　　　　　　　　　Ba - by,　slice it right;

LOVE AND HAPPINESS

Words and Music by AL GREEN
and MABON HODGES

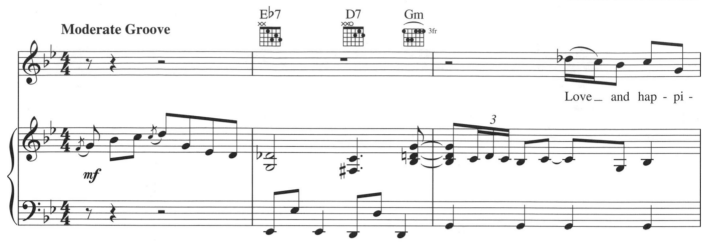

Moderate Groove

Love__ and hap - pi -

ness. Wait a min - ute! Some - thing's go - ing__ wrong,__ some - one's

on the phone,__ three o' - clock in the morn - ing,__ yeah.__ Talk - in'

Original key: G♯ minor. This edition has been transposed down one half-step to be more playable.

'bout how she can make it right, yeah. Well,

happiness is when you really

feel good a-bout some-bod-y, with noth-ing wrong. Be-ing in

love with some-one, yeah, yeah. Oh, ba-by,

love and hap - pi - ness.
(Love and hap - pi - ness.)

Love and hap - pi -

ness.
(Love and hap - pi - ness.)

Help me sing.

Love and hap - pi - ness.
(Love and hap - pi - ness.)
Love___ and hap - pi -

ness.
(Love and hap - pi - ness.)
Hey, hey,___

hey.___
Make you do right, yeah.___
ear - ly, oh.___

Love - 'll make you do wrong,___ yeah.
Make you stay out all night___ long.
Make you come home

Pow - er of love. *Lead vocal ad lib.*

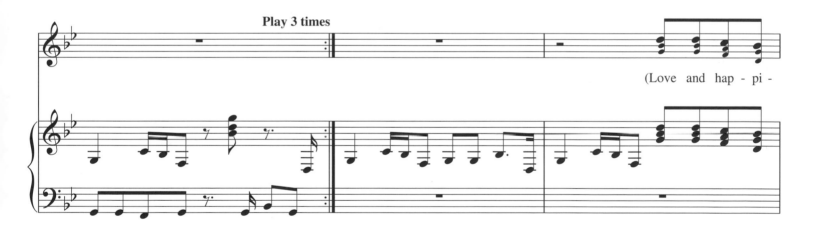

Play 3 times

(Love and hap - pi -

ness.)   (Love and hap - pi - ness.)

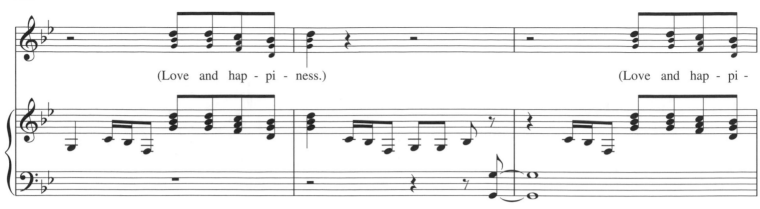

(Love and hap - pi - ness.)   (Love and hap - pi -

ness.)   Make you wan - na dance.

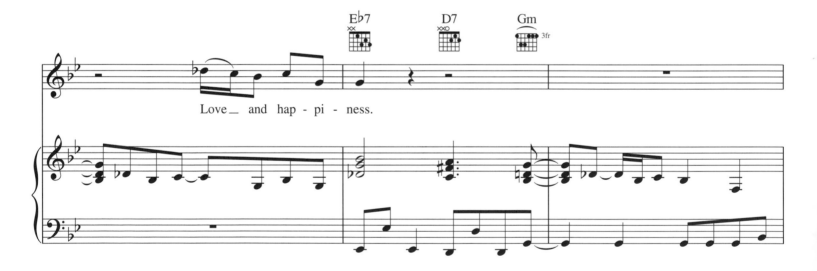

Love __ and hap - pi - ness.

Lead vocal ad lib.
(See additional lyrics)

Repeat and Fade

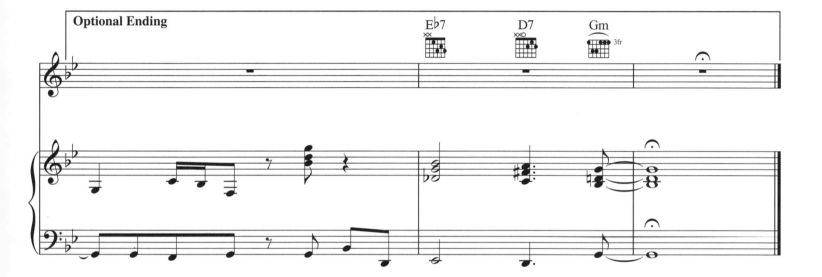

Additional Lyrics

Love is... wait a minute.
Love is...

Walkin' together,
Talkin' together,

Singin' together,
Playin' together.

Playin', wanna moan, say,
Mmm...

Moan for love.
Mmm...

Let me moan for love.
Mmm...

LOVE MACHINE

Words and Music by WARREN MOORE
and WILLIAM GRIFFIN

love ma-chine, __ and I won't work for no-bod-y but you. __

I'm just a love ma-chine, __ a hug-gin',

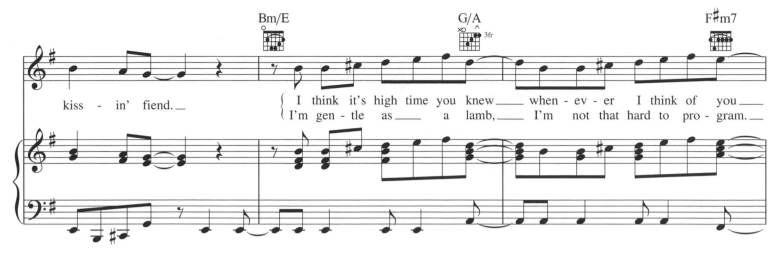

next to you. __ E - lec - tric - i - ty starts to flow, __
find out how __ to turn me on. __ Just set my dial __

and my in - di - ca - tor starts to glow, __ ooh!
and let me love you for a lit - tle while, __ ooh!

I'm just a

love ma - chine, __ and I won't work for no - bod - y but you. __

I'm just a love ma - chine, __ a hug - gin',

kiss - in' fiend. ___ La la la la la ___ la la la la ___

___ la la. ___ La la la la la ___

___ la la la la ___ la la. ___

I'm just a love ma - chine, ___

and I won't work for no-bod-y but you.____

I'm just a love ma - chine,____

Repeat and Fade

a hug - gin', kiss - in' fiend.____

Optional Ending

LOVE TO LOVE YOU, BABY

Words and Music by DONNA SUMMER,
GIORGIO MORODER and PETER BELLOTTE

love to love_you, ba - by.   I   love to love_you, ba - by.

Do it to me a - gain and a - gain,   you put me in such an aw - ful spin,_ in a spin.

LOVE ROLLERCOASTER

Words and Music by RALPH MIDDLEBROOKS,
JAMES WILLIAMS, MARSHALL JONES,
LEROY BONNER, CLARENCE SATCHELL,
WILLIE BECK and MARVIN R. PIERCE

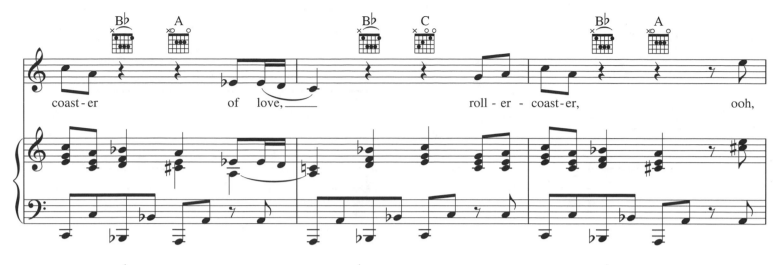

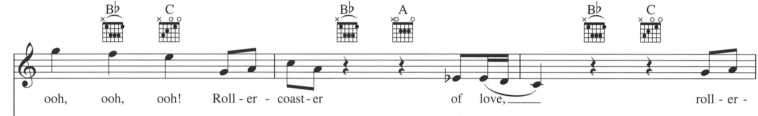

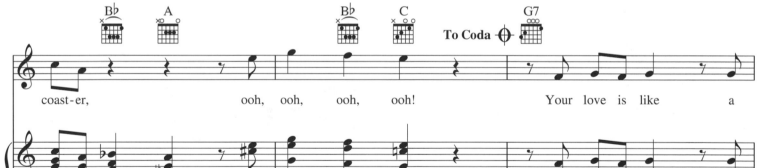

Your love is like a roll-er-coast-er, ba-by, ba-by.

All you do is ride, _____ ride! _____

Roll-er-

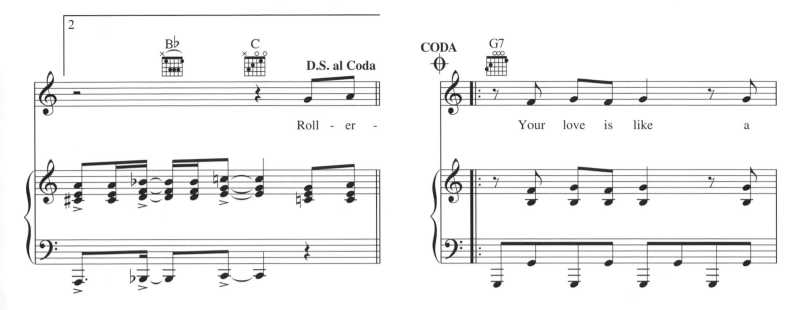

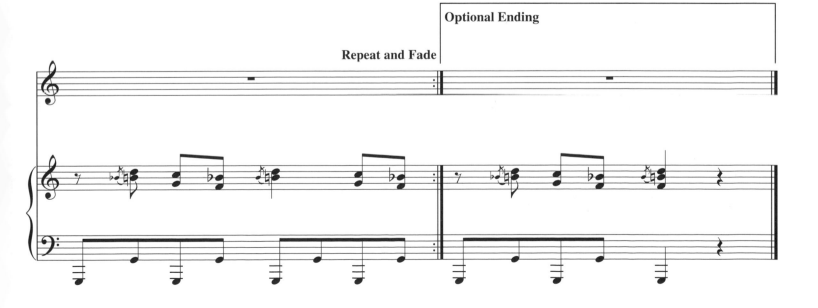

MACHO MAN

Words and Music by JACQUES MORALI, HENRI BELOLO,
VICTOR WILLIS and PETER WHITEHEAD

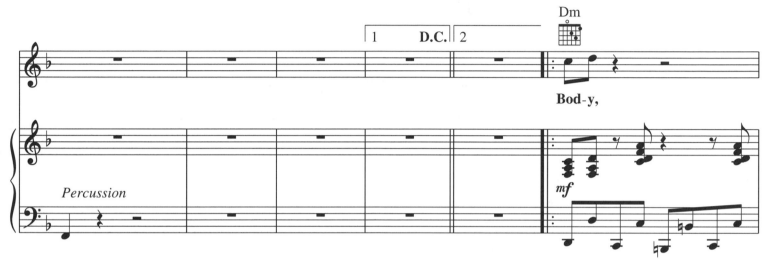

Additional Lyrics

D.C. Body, it's so hot, my body,
Body, love to pop my body.
Body, love to please my body.
Body, don't you tease my body.
Body, you'll adore my body.
Body, come explore my body.
Body, made by God, my body.
Body, it's so good, my body.

3. Ev'ry man ought to be a macho man.
To live a life of freedom machos make a stand.
Have their own life style and ideals.
Possess the strength and confidence life's a steal.
You can best believe that he's a macho man.
He's a special person in anybody's land.
To Chorus:

MAKE IT FUNKY, PT. 1

Words and Music by JAMES BROWN
and CHARLES FRED BOBBITT

NIGHTS ON BROADWAY

Words and Music by BARRY GIBB,
MAURICE GIBB and ROBIN GIBB

Moderately slow, with a strong beat

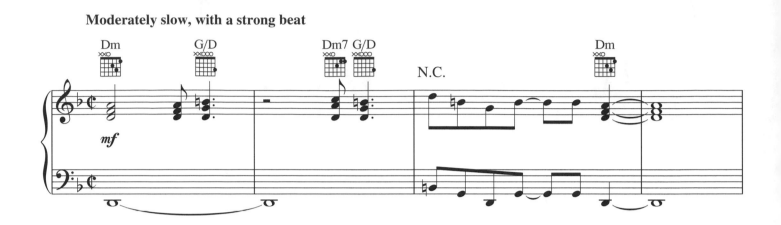

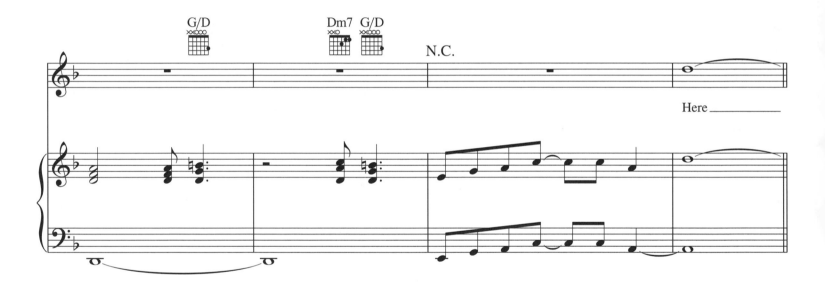

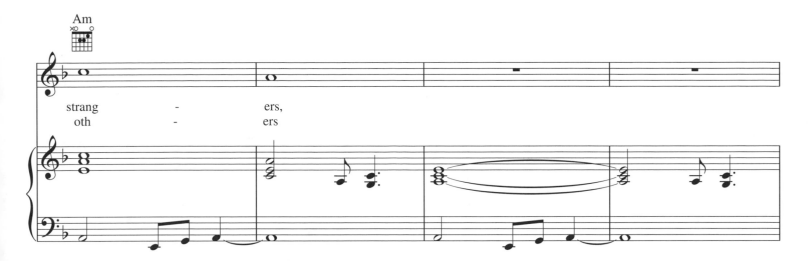

strang - - ers,
oth - - ers

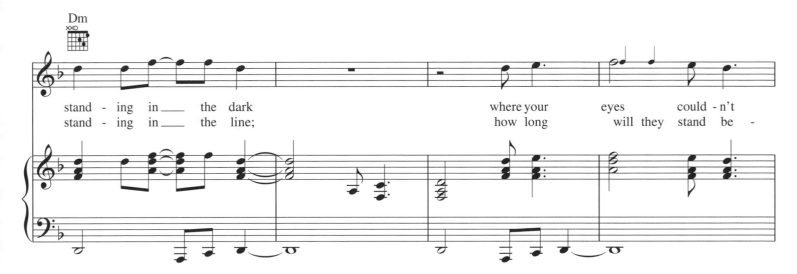

stand - ing in___ the dark   where your   eyes   could - n't
stand - ing in___ the line;   how long   will they   stand be -

see   me. }
tween   us? }   Well,   I   have___ to

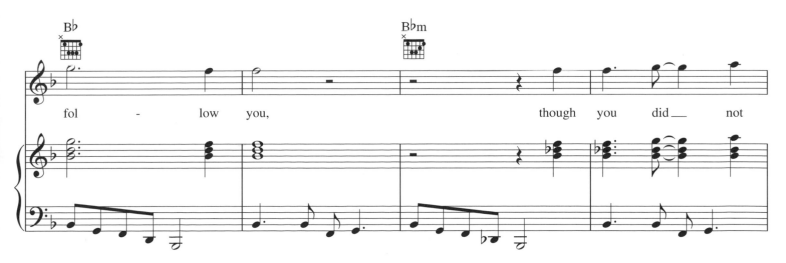

fol - low you,   though   you   did___ not

want me to. But that won't stop_ my

lov - in' you; __ I can't stay_ a-

way. _____ Blam - in' it all _____ on the nights_ on

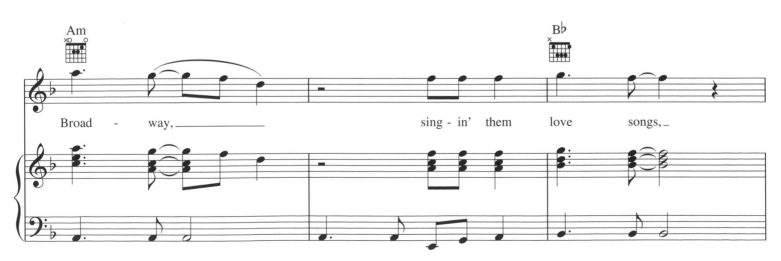

Broad - way, _____ sing - in' them love songs, _

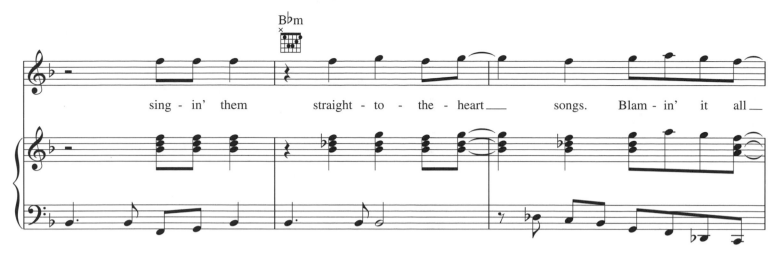

sing - in' them straight - to - the - heart ___ songs. Blam - in' it all ___

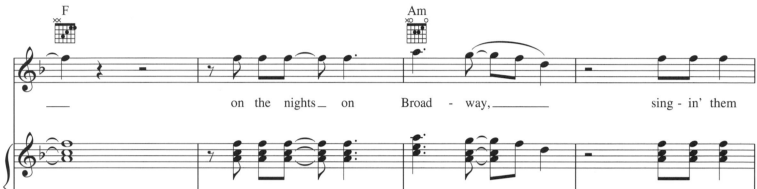

___ on the nights ___ on Broad - way, _____ sing - in' them

sweet sounds ___ to that cra - zy, cra - zy town. __

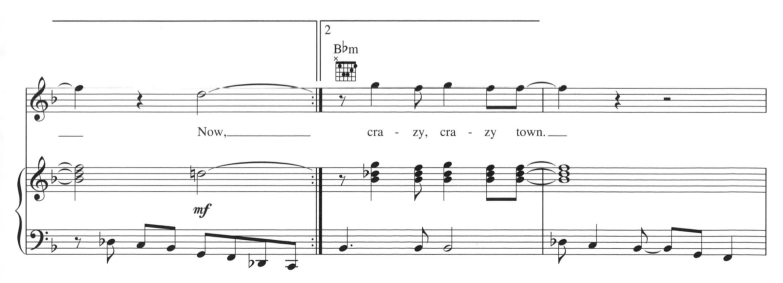

Now, _____ cra - zy, cra - zy town. __

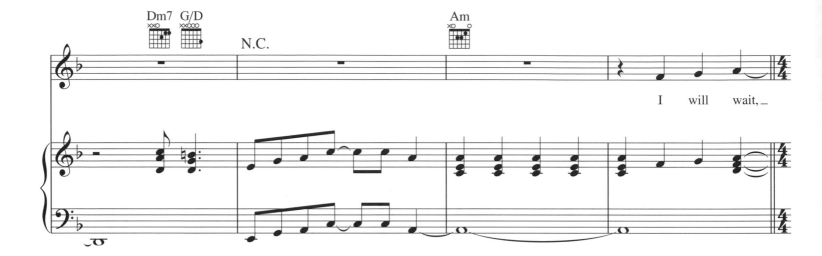

I will wait, __

e - ven if it takes for-

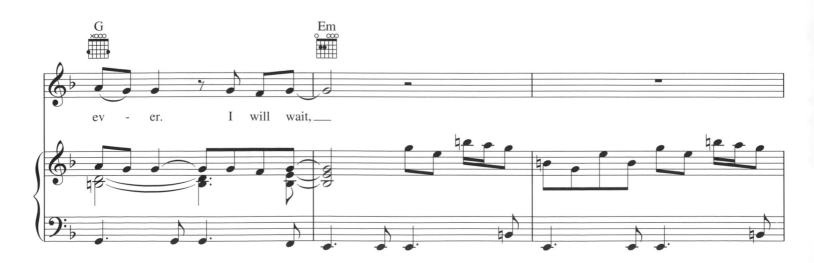

ev - er. I will wait, ___

e - ven if it takes a life - time. Some - how I feel in - side

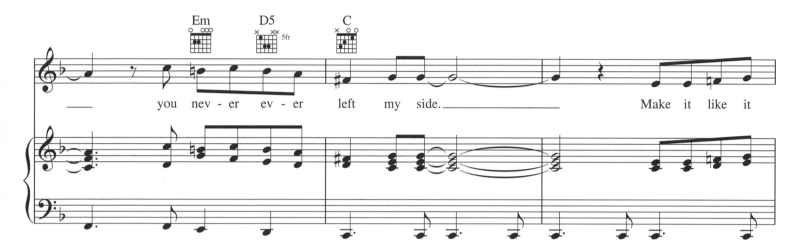

you nev - er ev - er left my side. Make it like it

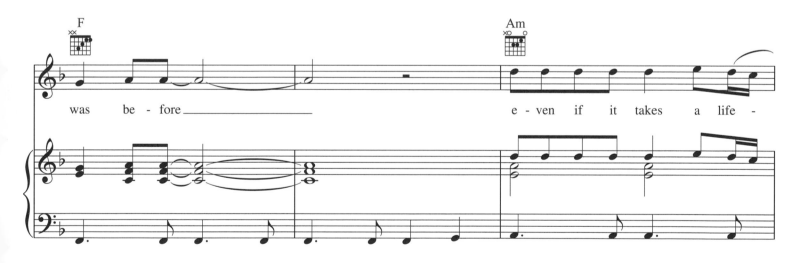

was be - fore e - ven if it takes a life -

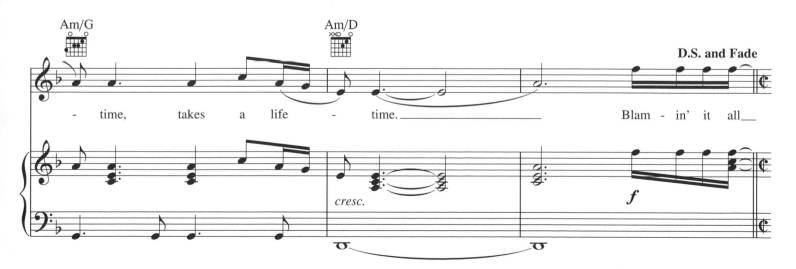

D.S. and Fade

- time, takes a life - time. Blam - in' it all

NO MORE TEARS
(Enough Is Enough)

Words and Music by PAUL JABARA
and BRUCE ROBERTS

Slowly

p legato

NO MORE TEARS

mp

C(add9)　B7+5　Bb13　A7　Dm7　Em7

It's rain-ing, it's pour-ing, my love life is bor-ing me to tears　af-ter all these

Fmaj9　G7-9　C(add9)　B7+5　Bb13　A7

years.　No sun-shine, no moon-light, no star-dust, no sign ___ of ro-

Dm7　Em7　Fmaj9　Bm7-5　E7+5(b9)　Am9

mance,　we don't stand a chance.　I al-ways dreamed I'd find the

mf

ENOUGH IS ENOUGH

you've had e-nough don't put up with his stuff, don't you do it.

If you've had your fill get the check, pay the bill, you can

ON THE RADIO

Words and Music by GIORGIO MORODER
and DONNA SUMMER

PAPA'S GOT A BRAND NEW BAG

Words and Music by
JAMES BROWN

Moderate Funk

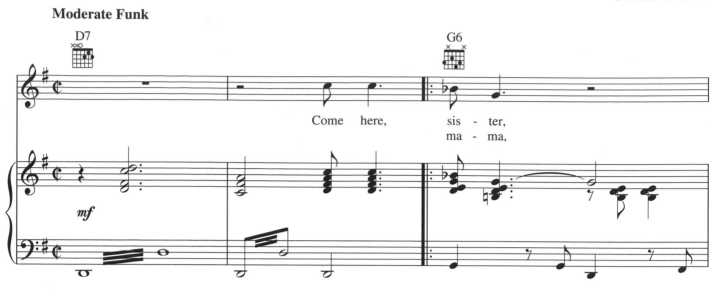

Come here, sis - ter,
ma - ma,

Pa - pa's in the swing.
and dig this cra - zy scene.

He ain't too
He's not too

hip
fan - cy

a - bout that new breed, babe.)
but this line is pret - ty clean.)

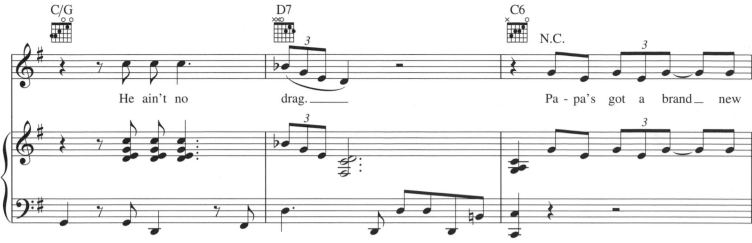

He ain't no drag.___ Pa-pa's got a brand__ new

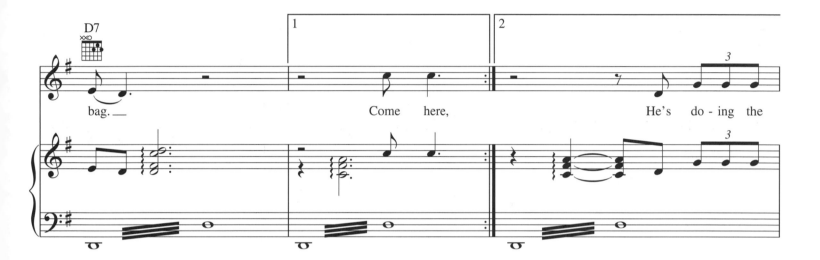

bag.___ |1. Come here, |2. He's do-ing the

Jerk. He's do-ing the Fly. Don't play him cheap 'cause you know he ain't

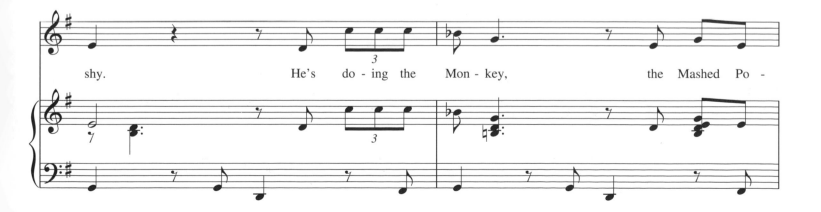

shy. He's do-ing the Mon-key, the Mashed Po -

ta - toes. Jump back, Jack, see you lat - er al - li - ga - tor. Come here,

sis - ter, Pa - pa's in the swing.

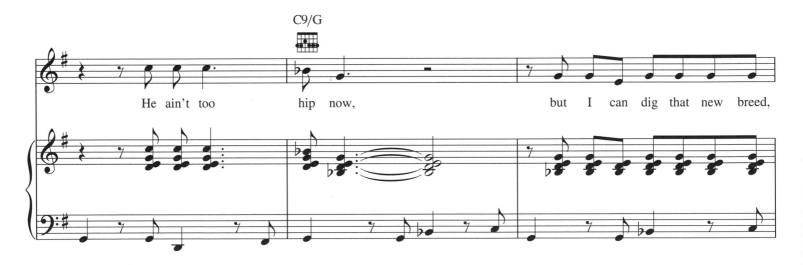

C9/G

He ain't too hip now, but I can dig that new breed,

G6

babe.

D7

He ain't no drag.

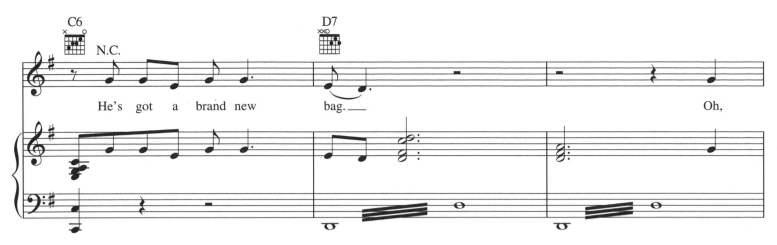

He's got a brand new bag.___ Oh,

Pa - pa, he's do - ing the Jerk. Pa - pa, he's do - ing the

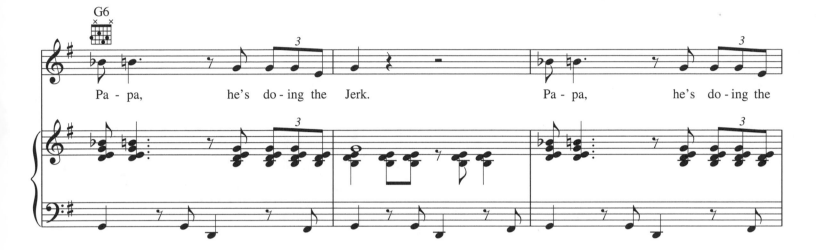

Jerk. He's do - ing the Twist just like this. He's do - ing the

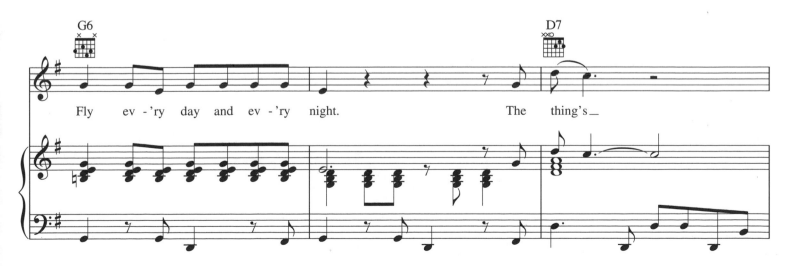

Fly ev - 'ry day and ev - 'ry night. The thing's__

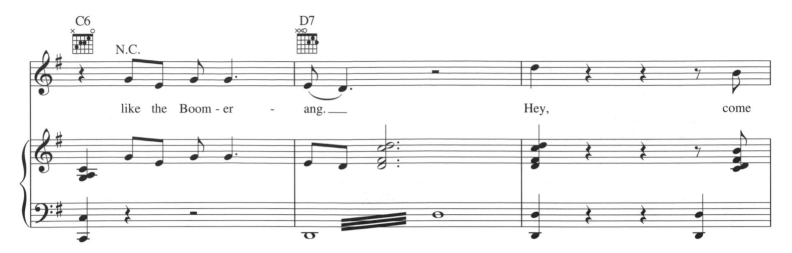

like the Boom-er - ang.___ Hey, come

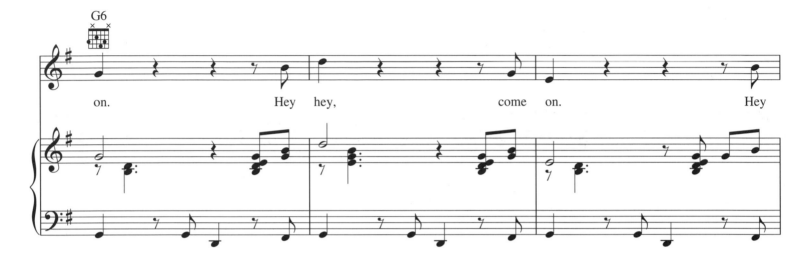

on. Hey hey, come on. Hey

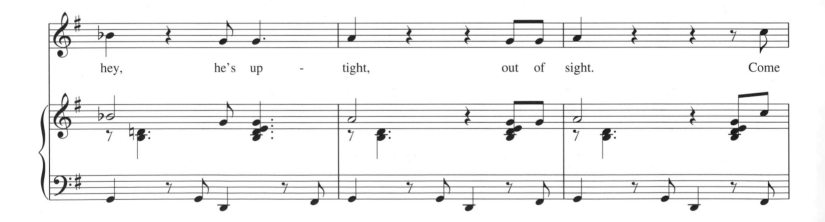

hey, he's up - tight, out of sight. Come

on. Hey! Hey!

PICK UP THE PIECES

Words and Music by JAMES HAMISH STUART,
ALAN GORRIE, ROGER BALL, ROBBIE McINTOSH,
OWEN McINTYRE and MALCOLM DUNCAN

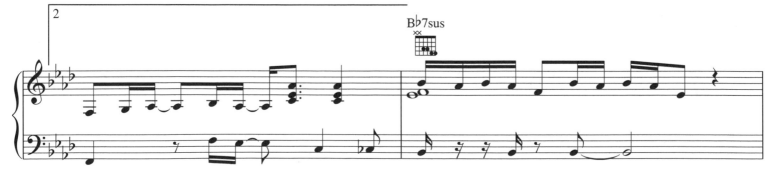

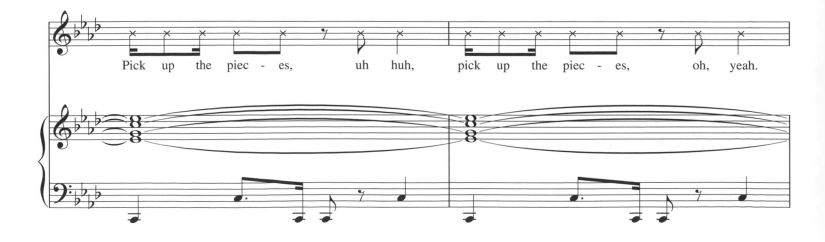

Pick up the piec - es, uh huh, pick up the piec - es, oh, yeah.

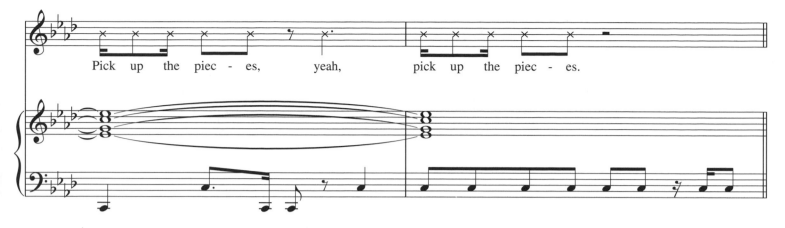

Pick up the piec - es, yeah, pick up the piec - es.

Bb7sus

Sax solo

D.S. al Coda

Pick up the

piec - es,   pick up the

piec - es.   Pick up the

ROCKIN' CHAIR

Words and Music by WILLIE JAMES CLARKE
and CLARENCE HENRY REID

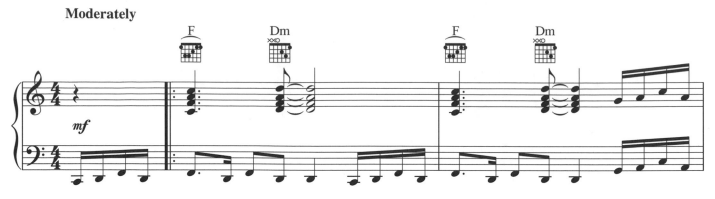

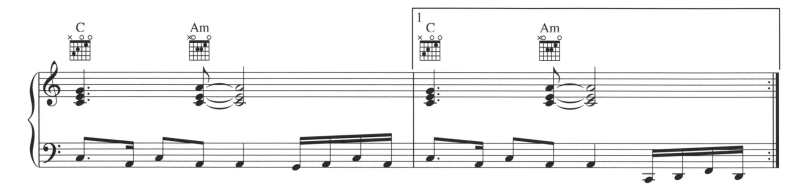

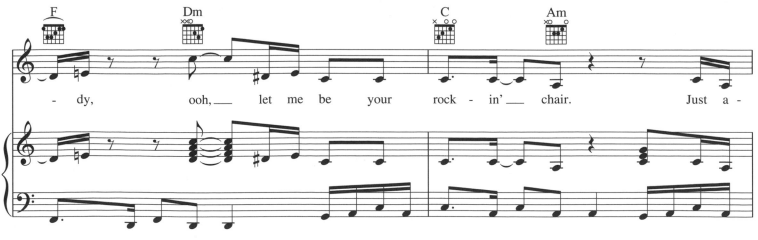

Sex-y ba-by, good lov-in' dad-dy, ooh,___ let me be your rock-in'___ chair. Just a-

rock me 'way___ from here.   Let's get it on.___   Come to me,

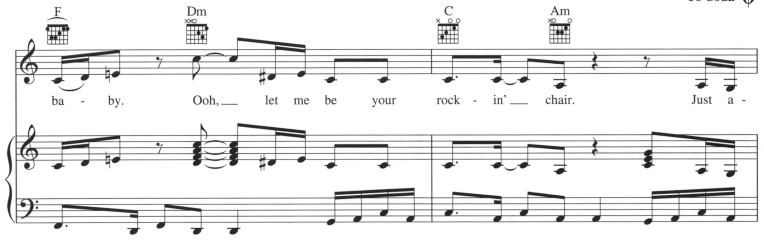

ba - by.   Ooh,___ let me be your   rock - in' ___ chair.   Just a -

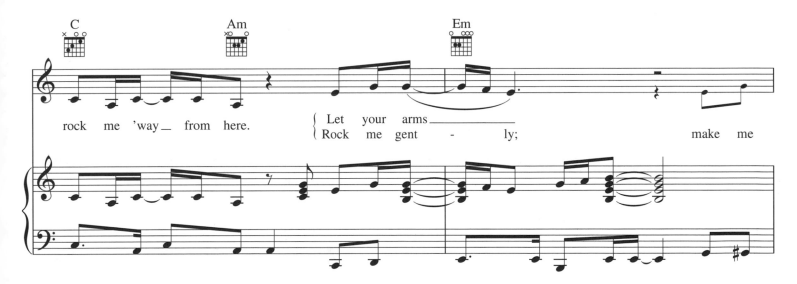

rock me 'way___ from here.   { Let your arms _____
                               { Rock me gent - ly;   make me

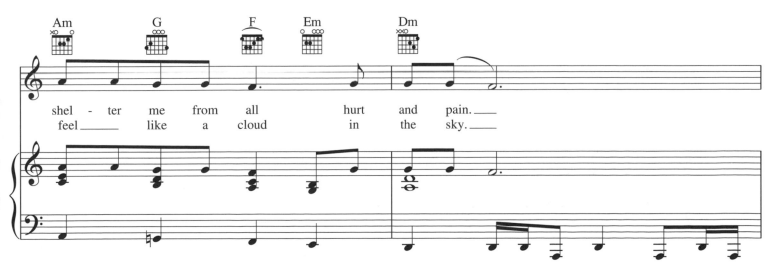

shel - ter me from all   hurt and pain.___
feel___ like a cloud   in the sky.___

Light my heart____
Whis - per soft - ly; let my

with your ev - er - last - in' flame.____
heart take wings____ and fly.____

Sex - y ba -

Sex - y ba -

D.S. al Coda

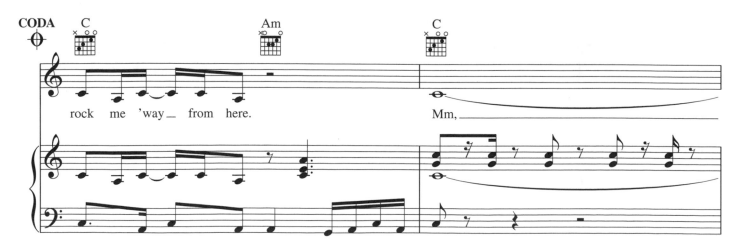

CODA

rock me 'way____ from here.

Mm,____

just a - rock me, ba - by, _____

ooh, in my rock - in' chair. _____ Ba -

- by, ___ ooh, ___ all night long 'til the morn - in' comes, just a -

you, ba - by. Ooh, _____

just rock, hon - ey, mm,

rock me, ba - by, _____ in the mid - night hour, _____ hey, in my

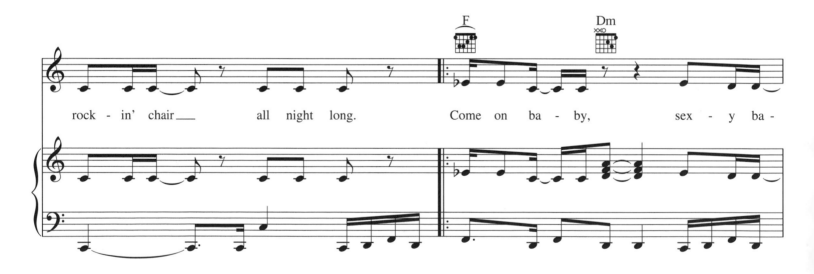

rock - in' chair _____ all night long. Come on ba - by, sex - y ba -

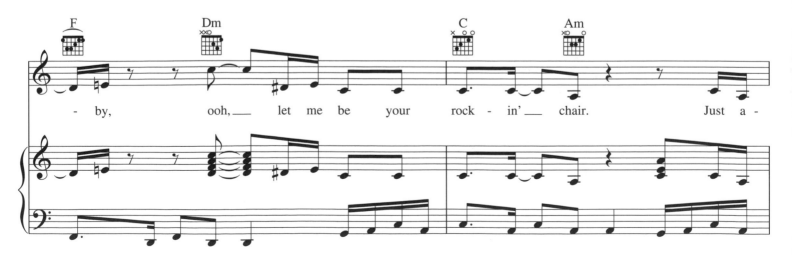

- by, ooh, _____ let me be your rock - in' _____ chair. Just a -

rock me 'way___ from here. Come on, ba - by, sex - y hon -

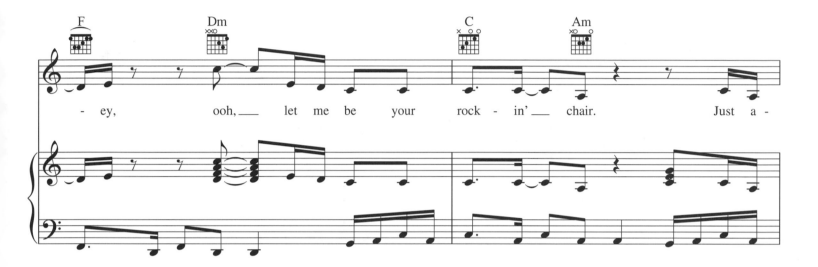

- ey, ooh,___ let me be your rock - in'___ chair. Just a -

Repeat and Fade

Optional Ending

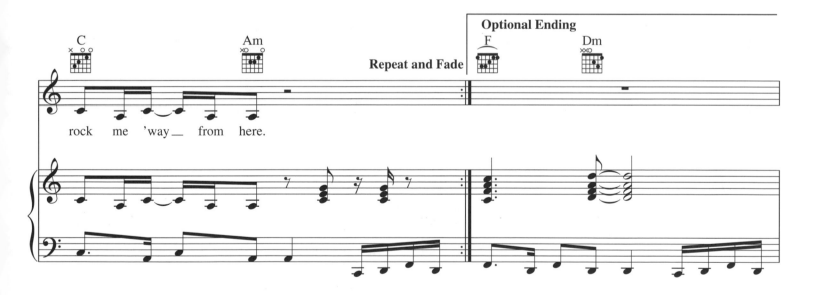

rock me 'way___ from here.

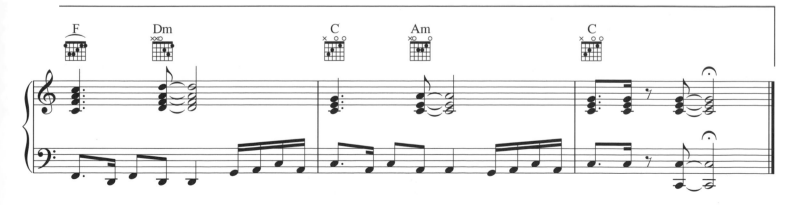

SHADOW DANCING

Words and Music by BARRY GIBB, ROBIN GIBB,
MAURICE GIBB and ANDY GIBB

You got me look-ing at that heav-en in your eyes. I was
All that I need is just one mo-ment in your arms. I was

chas-ing your di-rec-tion. I was tell-ing you no lies and I was
chas-ing your af-fec-tion. I was do-ing you no harm and I was

Do it light,   tak-ing me through the night.   Shad-ow danc - ing: ba - by, you

do it right.   Give me more.   Drag_ me a - cross the floor._   Shad-ow danc-

ing.   All _ this, and noth-ing more.

noth-ing more.

THEME FROM SHAFT

Words and Music by
ISAAC HAYES

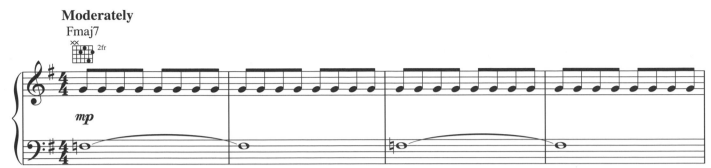

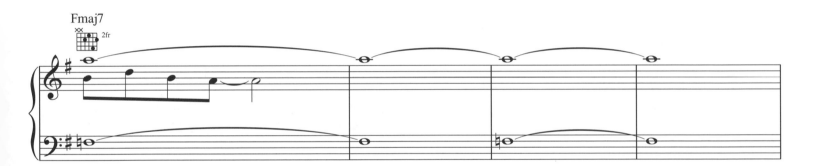

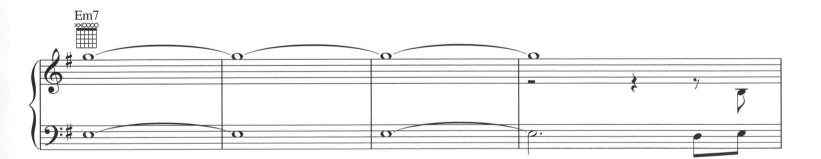

Spoken: Who's the black pri - vate dick _____ that's a sex ma - chine to all the chicks? (Shaft!)

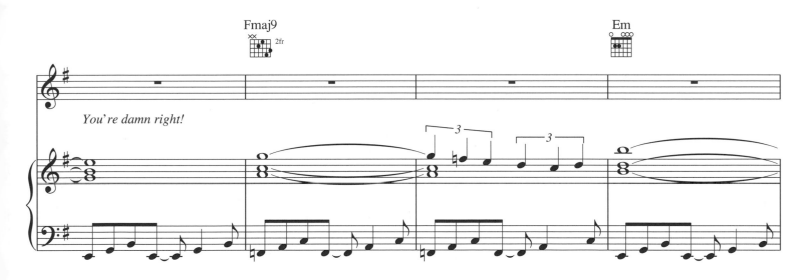

You're damn right!

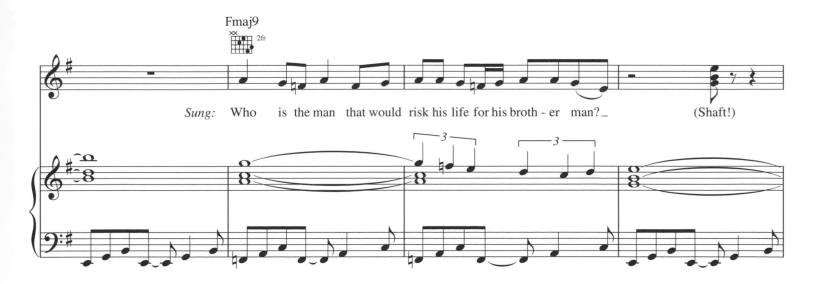

Sung: Who is the man that would risk his life for his broth - er man? _ (Shaft!)

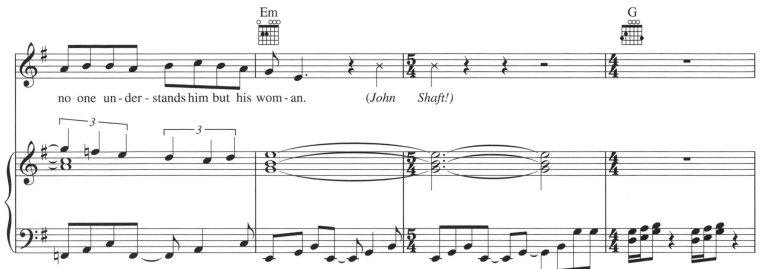

no one un-der-stands him but his wom-an. (*John   Shaft!*)

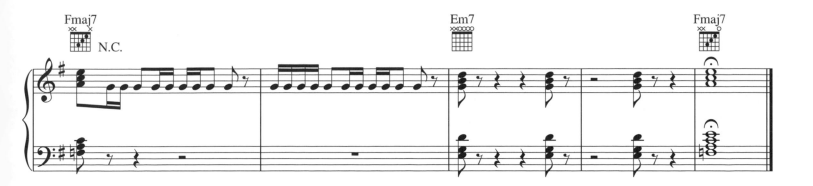

SHAME

Words and Music by JOHN FITCH
and REUBEN CROSS

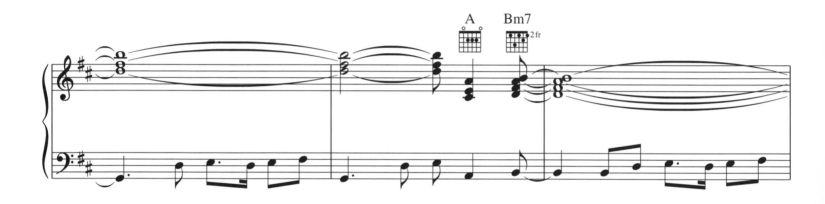

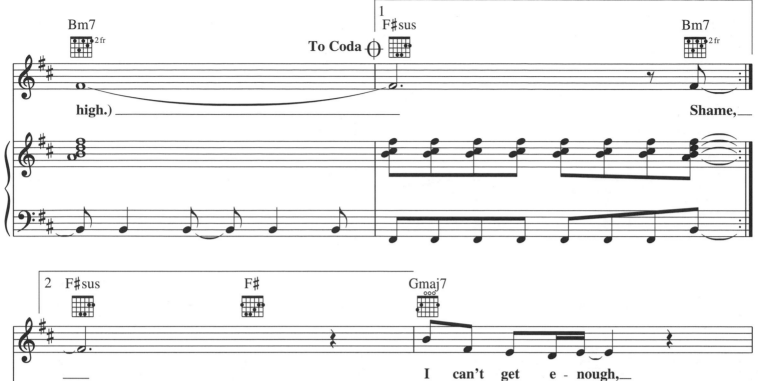

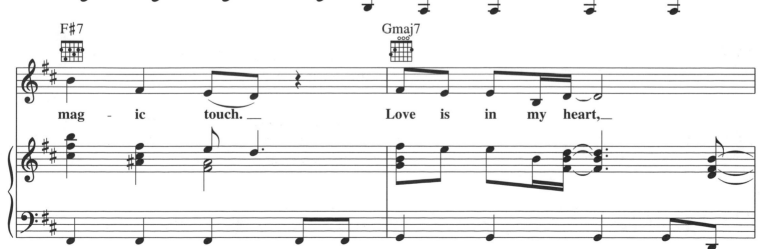

SHINING STAR

Words and Music by MAURICE WHITE,
PHILIP BAILEY and LARRY DUNN

STAYIN' ALIVE

from the Motion Picture SATURDAY NIGHT FEVER

Words and Music by BARRY GIBB,
MAURICE GIBB and ROBIN GIBB

Well, you can tell—

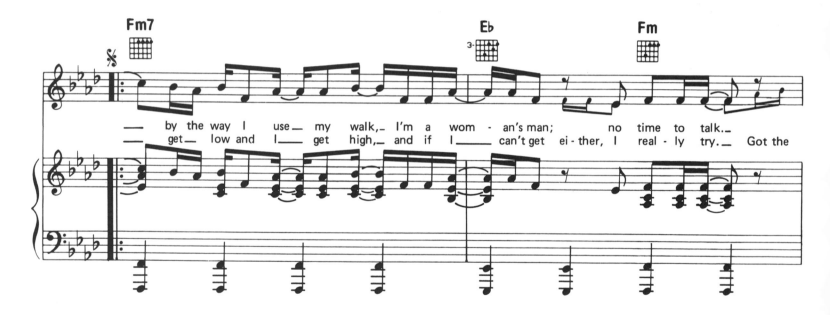

— by the way I use— my walk,— I'm a wom-an's man; no time to talk.—
— get low and I get high,— and if I can't get ei-ther, I real-ly try.— Got the

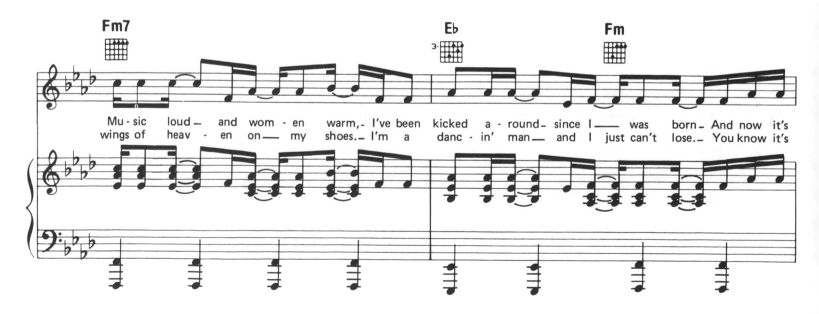

Mu-sic loud— and wom-en warm,— I've been kicked a-round— since I— was born. And now it's
wings of heav-en on— my shoes.— I'm a danc-in' man— and I just can't lose.— You know it's

SUPER FREAK

Words and Music by RICK JAMES
and ALONZO MILLER

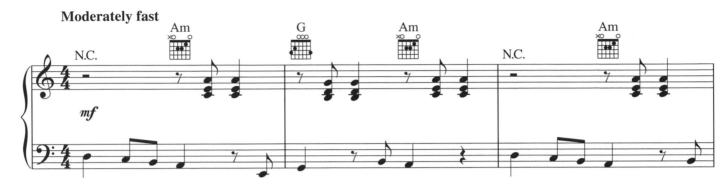

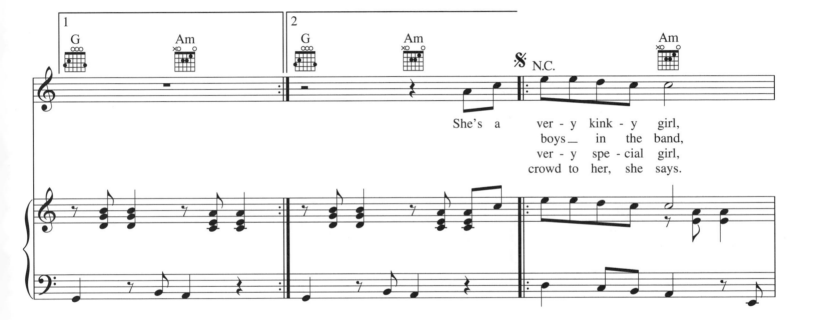

She's a ver - y kink - y girl,
boys___ in the band,
ver - y spe - cial girl,
crowd to her, she says.

the kind you don't take home to Moth - er.
she says that I'm her all - time fa - v'rite.
from her head down to her toe - nails.
"Room sev - en four - teen; I'll be wait - ing."

She will
When I
And she'll
When I

never let your spir-its down,_____ once you get her off___ the street.
make my move to her room, it's the right time; she's nev-er hard__ to please.
wait for me at back-stage with her girl-friends in a lim - ou - sine.
get there she's got in-cense, wine and can - dles; it's such a freak - y scene.

She likes the That girl is pret-ty wild__ now. (The
Three's not a girl is pret-ty kink - y. (The

girl's a su - per freak.) The kind of girl you read a-bout (in
girl's a su - per freak.) I real-ly love to taste her

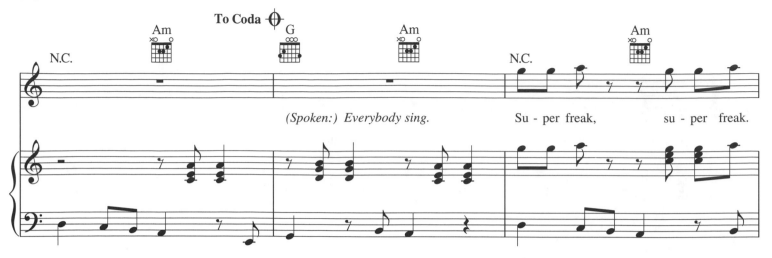

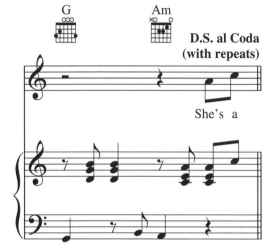

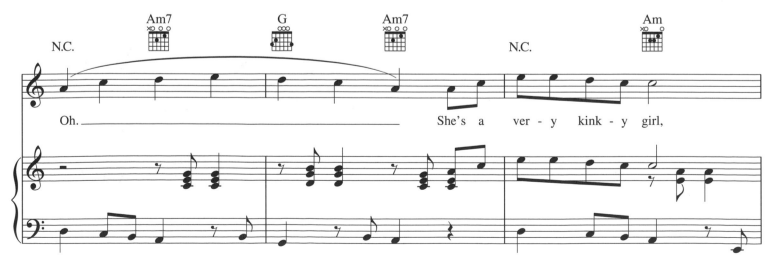

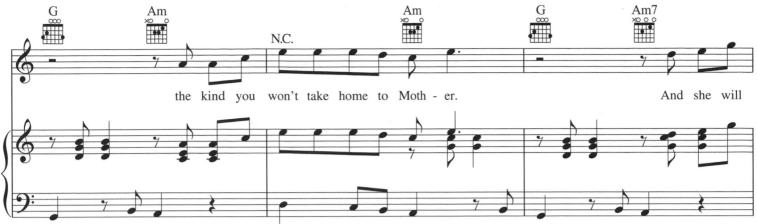

the kind you won't take home to Moth - er. And she will

nev - er let your spir - its down, _____ once you get her off ____ the street.

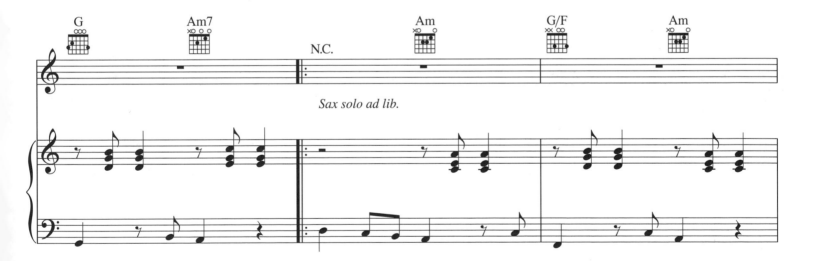

Sax solo ad lib.

Repeat and Fade

Optional Ending

SUPERSTITION

Words and Music by
STEVIE WONDER

(1., 3.) Thir-teen month old ba-
(2.) Keep me in a day-

- by broke the look-ing glass.
- dream. Keep me go-in' strong.

Sev - en years of bad
You don't wan - na save

luck. The good things in your past.
me. Sad is my song.

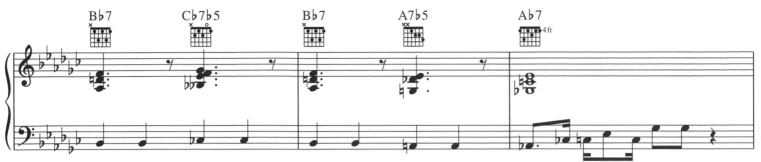

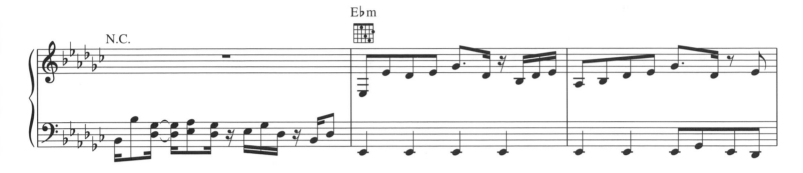

Ver - y su - per - sti -

Su - per - sti - tion ain't the way. _____

(vocal 1st time only)

CODA

Repeat and Fade

Optional Ending

THAT'S THE WAY
(I Like It)

Words and Music by HARRY WAYNE CASEY
and RICHARD FINCH

Do do__ do__ do do do do do__ do.__ Do do__ do__ do do do

do do__ do.__ That's the way (uh - huh, uh - huh) I like it. (uh - huh, uh - huh)

That's the way (uh - huh, uh - huh) I like it. (uh - huh, uh - huh)

Thats the way (uh - huh, uh - huh) I like it. (uh - huh, uh - huh)

To Coda ⊕

That's the way (uh - huh, uh - huh) I like it. (uh - huh, uh - huh)

Fm7

When you take me ___ by the hand, ___
When I get to ___ be in your arms, ___

tell me I'm ___ your lov - in' man.
when we're all, ___ all a - lone.

When you give__ me__ all your love and
When you whis - per__ sweet in my ear, and

D.S. al Coda

do it, babe,_ the ver - y best you can. Oh.
when you turn,_ turn me on. Oh.

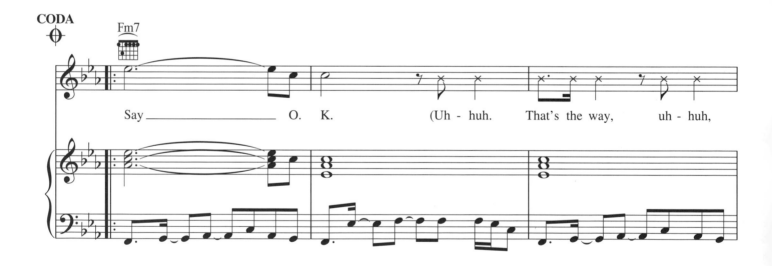

CODA

Fm7

Say__ O. K. (Uh - huh. That's the way, uh - huh,

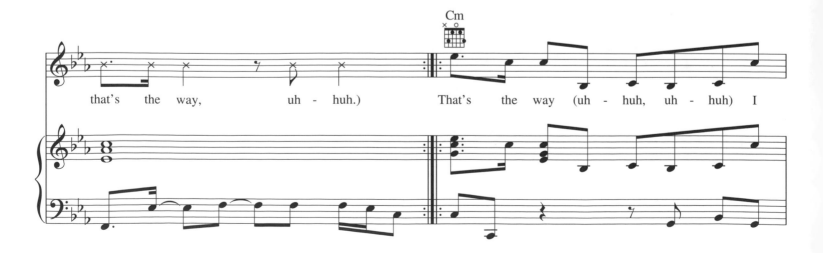

Cm

that's the way, uh - huh.) That's the way (uh - huh, uh - huh) I

like it. (uh - huh, uh - huh) That's the way (uh - huh, uh - huh) I like it. (uh - huh, uh - huh)

Do do___ do___ do do do do do___ do.___ Do do___ do___ do do do

do do___ do.___ That's the way (uh - huh, uh - huh) I like it. (uh - huh, uh - huh)

Repeat and Fade

Optional Ending

That's the way (uh - huh, uh - huh) I like it. (uh - huh, uh - huh) like it.

THIS WILL BE
(An Everlasting Love)

Moderately bright rock

Words and Music by MARVIN YANCY
and CHUCK JACKSON

TURN THE BEAT AROUND

Words and Music by PETER JACKSON JR.
and GERALD JACKSON

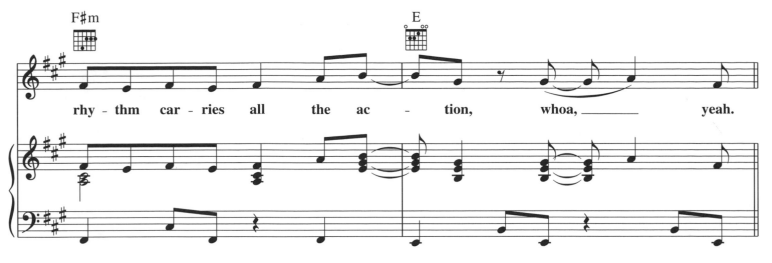

rhy - thm car - ries all the ac - tion, whoa, _____ yeah.

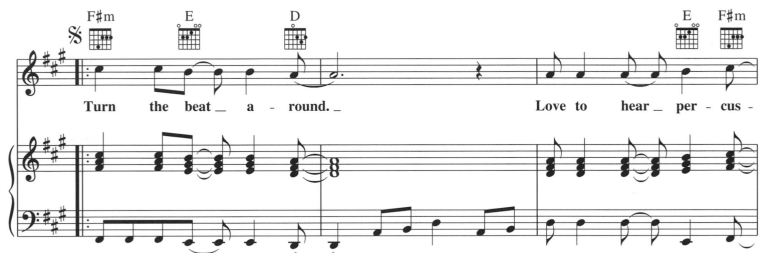

Turn the beat __ a - round. __ Love to hear __ per - cus -

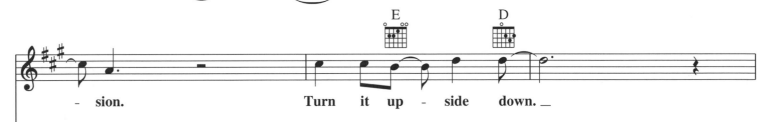

- sion. Turn it up - side down. __

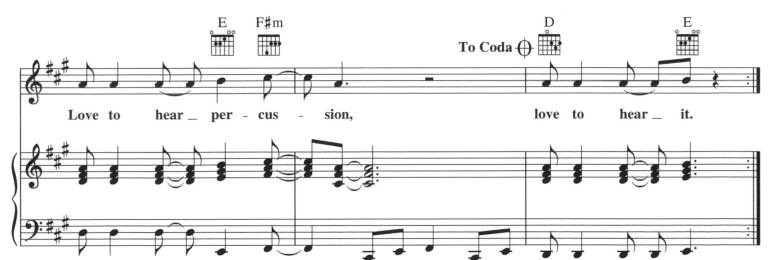

Love to hear __ per - cus - sion, love to hear __ it.

Well, the gui-tar play-er starts play-ing with the syn-co-pat-ed rhy-thm, scratch, scratch, _ scratch

makes _ me want to move my bod - y, yeah, yeah, _ yeah. _

And when the drum-mer starts beat-ing that beat he nails that beat with the syn-co-pat-ed rhy-thm and the

rat - tat - tat - tat - tat - tat on the drums, _ hey, _____ yeah.

no chord

D.S. al Coda

love to hear ___ it, love to hear ___ it,

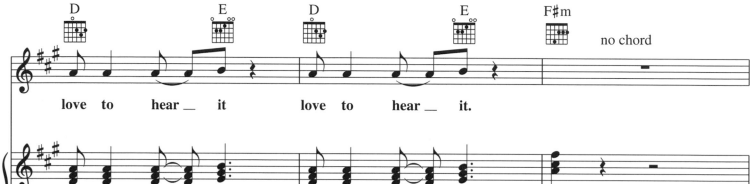

love to hear ___ it love to hear ___ it.

no chord

Play 3 times

Turn it up, turn it up, turn it up - side down.

WE ARE FAMILY

Words and Music by NILE RODGERS
and BERNARD EDWARDS

WHIP IT

Words and Music by MARK MOTHERSBAUGH
and GERALD CASALE

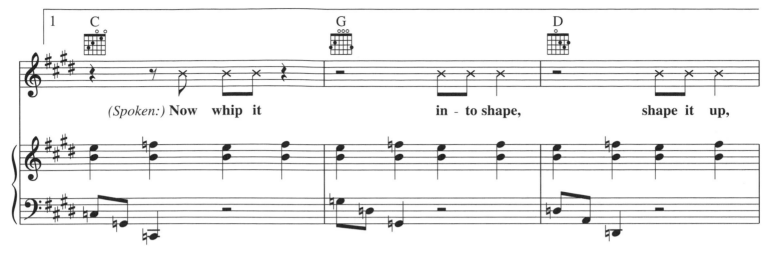

(Spoken:) **Now whip it** in - to shape, shape it up,

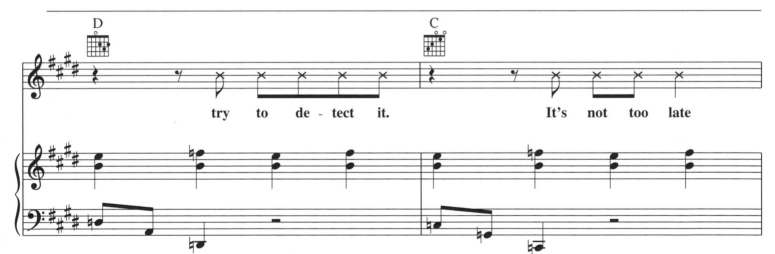

get straight, go for-ward, move a-head.

try to de-tect it. It's not too late

to whip it, whip it good.

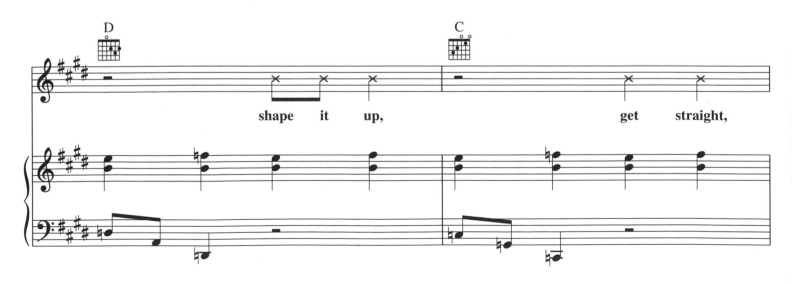

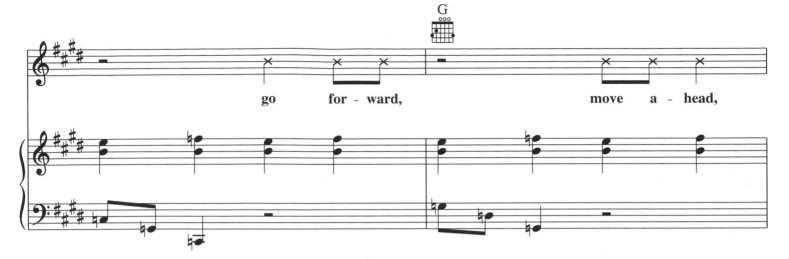

go for - ward, move a - head,

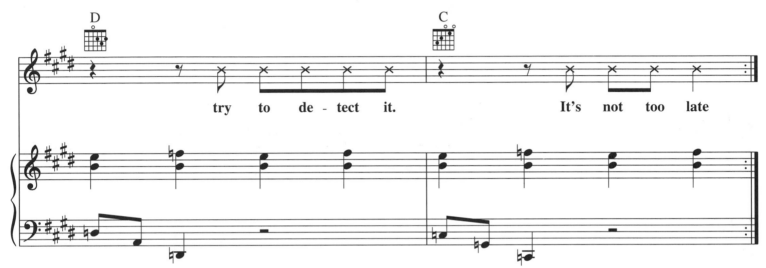

try to de - tect it. It's not too late

to whip it, whip it good.

WHAT IS HIP?

Words and Music by STEPHEN KUPKA, EMILIO CASTILLO
and DAVID GARIBALDI

So you want to jump out your trick bag and
came a part of the new breed, been
went and found you a gu-ru in an

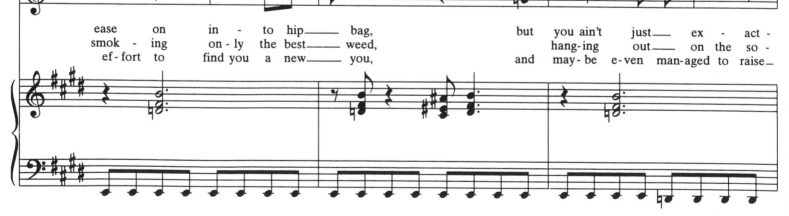

ease on in-to hip bag, but you ain't just ex-act-ly
smok-ing on-ly the best weed, hang-ing out on the so-
ef-fort to find you a new you, and may-be e-ven man-aged to raise

ly   sure___ what's   hip.___   You
called   hip - pest   set.___   Be - ing
___ your con - scious lev - el.   While you're

start- ed   to let___ your   hair___ grow,   spend   big   bucks to cop you a   ward-
seen   in   all___ the right plac - es,   seen   with___ just the right fac -
striv-ing to find___ the right road,___   there's   one   thing___ you should know:___

robe,   but some - how you know there's   much   more   to   the trip.___
es,   you should be   sat - is - fied, but still it ain't   quite right.___
___   what's hip to- day   might be - come   pas - sé.___

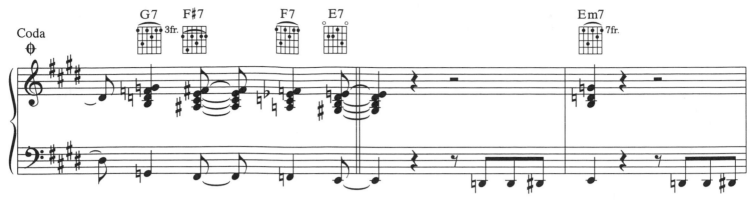

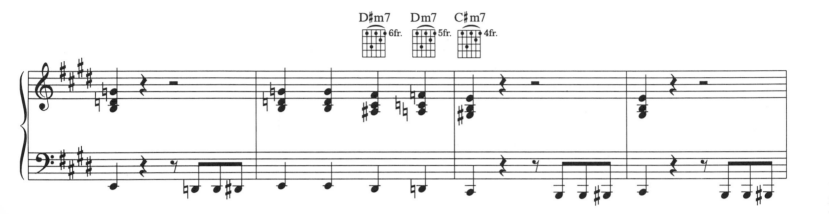

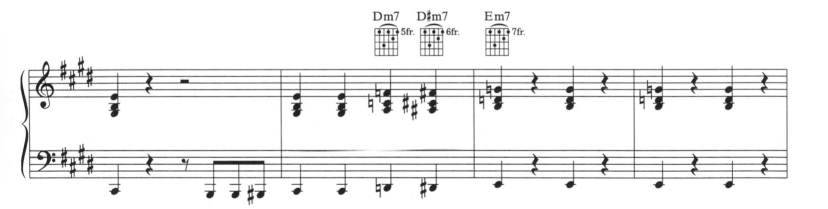

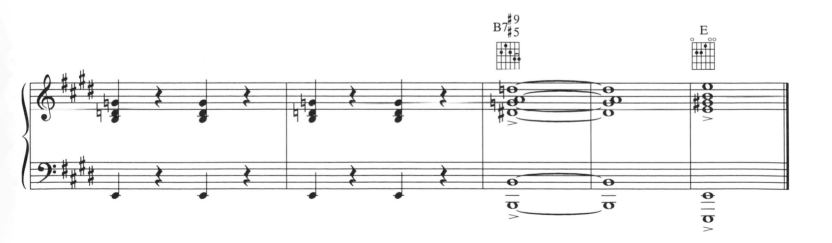

WILL IT GO ROUND IN CIRCLES

Words and Music by BILLY PRESTON
and BRUCE FISHER

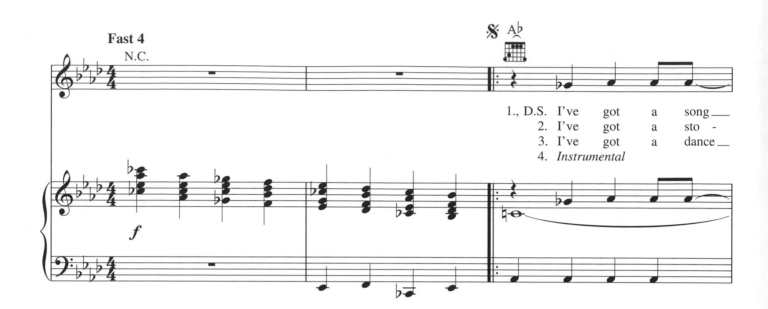

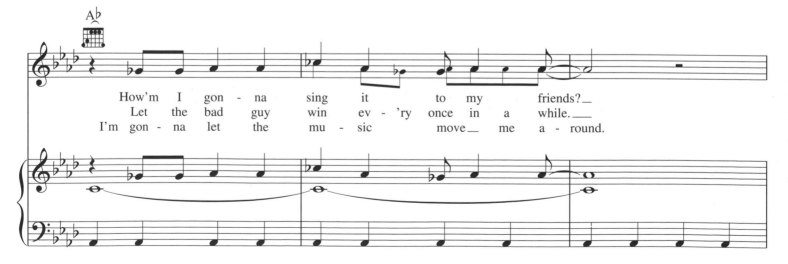

I've got a song,___ I ain't got no
I've got a sto - ry, ain't got no
I've got a dance,___ I ain't got no

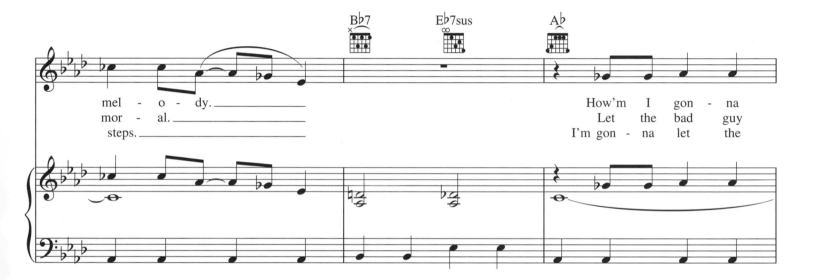

mel - o - dy._____
mor - al._____
steps._____

How'm I gon - na
Let the bad guy
I'm gon - na let the

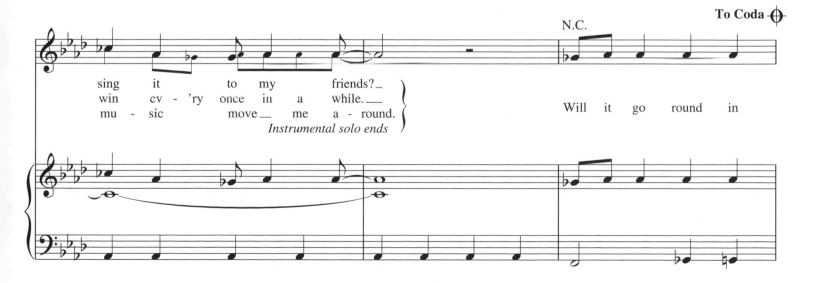

sing it to my friends?___
win ev - 'ry once in a while.___
mu - sic move___ me a - round.

Instrumental solo ends

Will it go round in

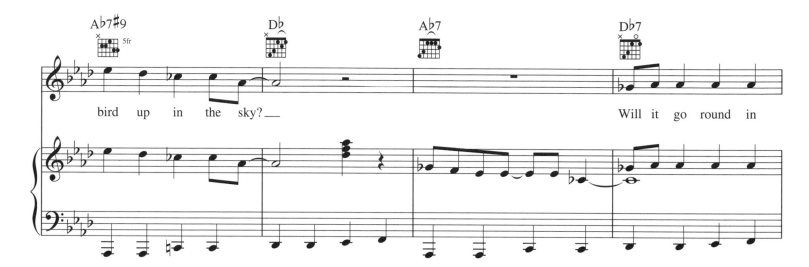

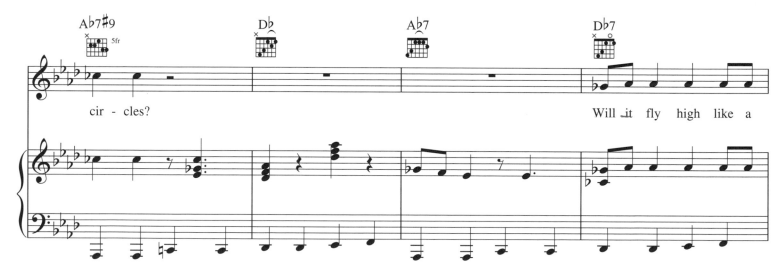

Y.M.C.A.

Words and Music by JACQUES MORALI,
HENRI BELOLO and VICTOR WILLIS

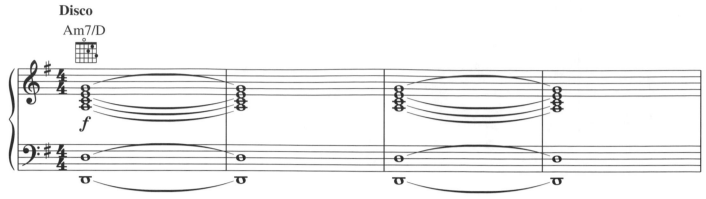

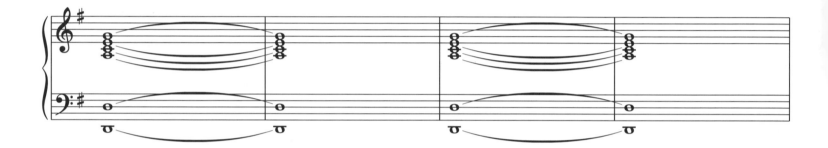

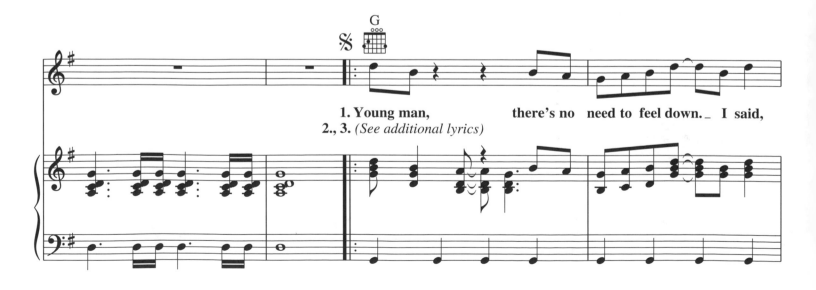

1. Young man,   there's no   need to feel down. _   I said,
2., 3. *(See additional lyrics)*

Em

young man,   pick your-self off the ground. __ I said,

C

young man,   'cause you're in a new town __ there's no

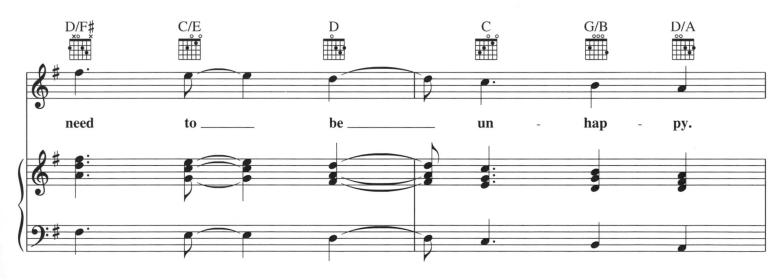

D/F♯   **C/E**   **D**   **C**   **G/B**   **D/A**

need   to _____ be _____ un - hap - py.

G

Young man,   there's a place you can go, ____ I said,

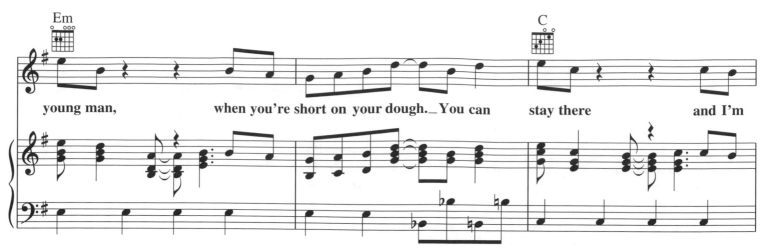

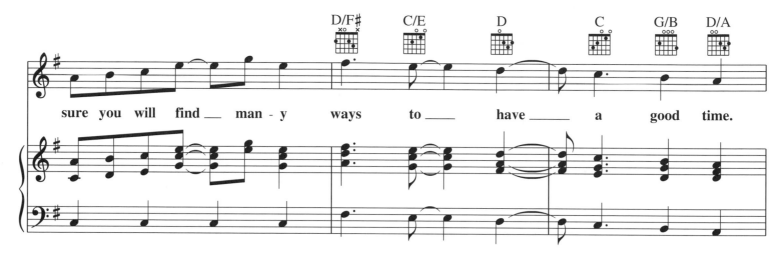

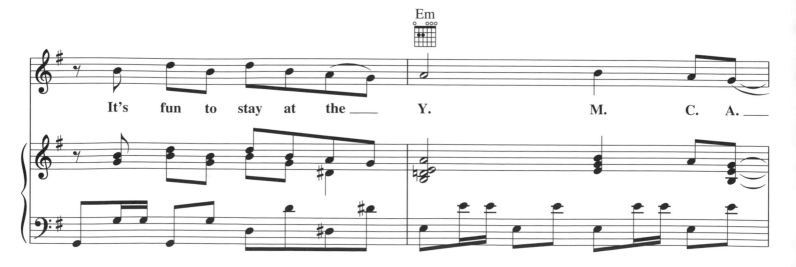

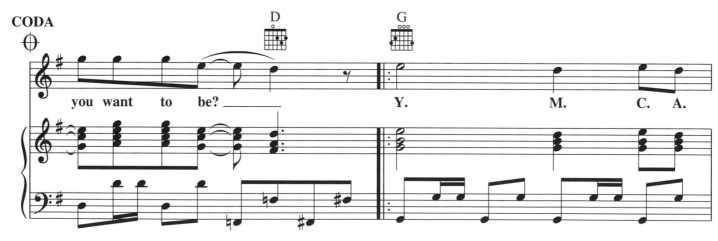

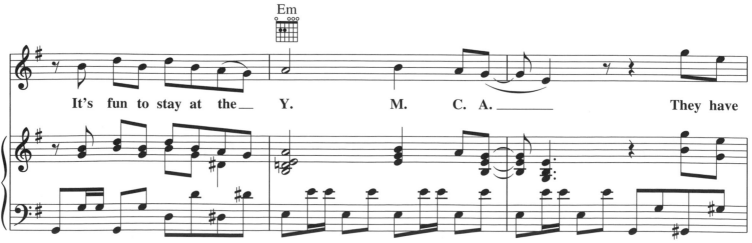

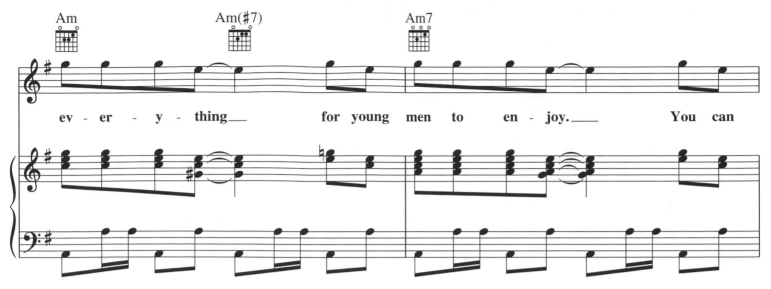

ev - er - y - thing___ for young men to en - joy.___ You can

Repeat ad lib. and Fade

hang out with all ___ the boys. ___ It's fun to stay at the

Additional Lyrics

2. Young man, are you listening to me?
   I said, young man what do you want to be?
   I said, young man you can make real your dreams
   But you've got to know this one thing.

   No man does it all by himself.
   I said young man put your pride on the shelf.
   And just go there to the Y.M.C.A.
   I'm sure they can help you today.
   To Chorus:

3. Young man, I was once in your shoes
   I said, I was down and out and with the blues.
   I felt no man cared if I were alive.
   I felt the whole world was so jive.

   That's when someone come up to me
   And said, "Young man, take a walk up the street.
   It's a place there called the Y.M.C.A.
   They can start you back on your way."
   To Chorus:

YOU MAKE ME FEEL LIKE DANCING

Words and Music by VINI PONCIA
and LEO SAYER

danc - ing, __ danc - ing, __ dance the night __ a - way. I feel like

danc - ing, __ danc - ing, __ ah. _____

And if you'll let me stay, we'll dance our lives a - way.

YOU SEXY THING

Words and Music by
E. BROWN

YOU SHOULD BE DANCING

from SATURDAY NIGHT FEVER

Words and Music by BARRY GIBB,
MAURICE GIBB and ROBIN GIBB